THE THIRD WORLD

LATIN AMERICA

THE THIRD WORLD SERIES

 AFRICA

 LATIN AMERICA

 MIDDLE EAST

 SOUTH ASIA

 SOUTHEAST ASIA

THE THIRD WORLD

LATIN AMERICA

Philip Evanson

The Dushkin Publishing Group, Inc.
Guilford, Connecticut 06437

Library of Congress Catalog Card Number: 84-93314
Manufactured in the United States of America

First Printing

CONTENTS

LATIN
AMERICA

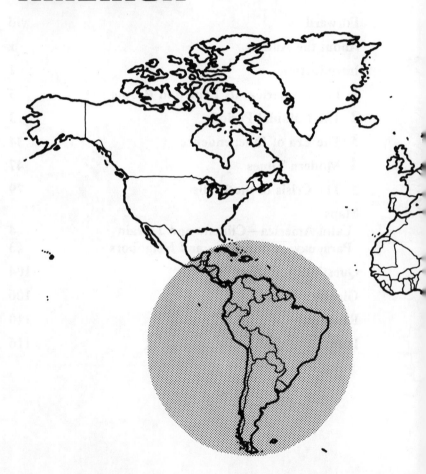

THE THIRD WORLD

FOREWORD

THE THIRD WORLD has been written to provide much needed materials on non-Western cultures. In the past, most studies of the non-Western world were chronological in organization or dealt with the regions studied by using the traditional themes of religion, politics, history, and so on. Very few, if any, offered the student a thematic perspective.

THE THIRD WORLD discusses the regions of Africa, Latin America, Middle East, South Asia, and Southeast Asia from the perspective of societies and cultures in transition. This has been done in a variety of ways: by focusing on the problems of new nations struggling with the issues of economic development; by organizing the study around the major minorities of a region; by investigating the ways in which traditional norms and modern forms interact; and by seeing the problems of modern non-American cultures in the light of the anxieties, conflicts, and tensions of our society.

In their own ways, the authors of each of the volumes have attempted to make their regions come alive. The authors teach subjects related to the region about which they have written, and all have spent considerable time there. Consequently, they have a deep appreciation for the peoples with whom they have worked, and the cultures in which they have lived. The authors are sensitive to the need for developing a knowledge of their areas which are intelligible to young Americans, but which, at the same time, are region-centric rather than Euro- or America-centric. The significance of such a perspective is illustrated by two plaques on a nineteenth century Spanish monument on the island of Mactan in the

Philippines glorifying God, Spain, the Queen Regent then in power, and Ferdinand Magellan. In 1941 a historical marker titled, "Ferdinand Magellan's Death" was anchored into the monument stating, "On this spot Ferdinand Magellan died on April 27, 1521, wounded in an encounter with the soldiers of Lapulapu, Chief of Mactan island. One of Magellan's ships, the Victoria, under the command of Juan Sebastian Elcano, sailed from Cebu on May 1, 1521, and anchored at San Lucar de Barrameda on September 6, 1522, thus completing the first circumnavigation of the earth." Ten years later, in 1951, the newly independent Republic of the Philippines erected a second marker entitled "Lapulapu." It read, "Here, on 27 April 1521, Lapulapu and his men repulsed the Spanish invaders, killing their leader Ferdinand Magellan. Thus, Lapulapu became the first Filipino to have repelled European aggression."

The authors of the volumes of THE THIRD WORLD are not only interested in these countries from an academic point of view. They also hope to be able to make a contribution to world understanding and world peace by increasing your knowledge of non-Western cultures, peoples, and societies.

THE THIRD WORLD has, in short, been written with a sense of urgency and a sense of mission. The urgency is the chaotic state of today's world. The mission is knowledge, not the kind of knowledge that comes from memorizing facts, but the understanding that comes from dispelling myths and from grappling with problems relevant to you and the world in which you live. You have a stake in the future of the world. It's a rapidly shrinking world in which the problems of the Third World are your problems. It's up to you to try to solve them. We hope that THE THIRD WORLD will be of some help along the way.

—**Donald K. Swearer**
Editorial Advisor
Third World Series
Swathmore College

ABOUT THE AUTHOR

Philip Evanson received his Ph.D. in Latin American history from the University of Virginia. Since 1967, he has held teaching positions at Temple University and the University of Illinois at Chicago Circle. He has visited or lived in ten Latin American nations and has taught at the University of Santa Ursula in Rio de Janeiro, Brazil.

INTRODUCTION

In recent years, news coming out of Latin America has generally been bad. The Central American nations of El Salvador, Guatemala, and Nicaragua either passed or were passing through highly destructive and murderous civil wars. The worldwide economic recession of the late 1970s struck hard and stopped, or even reversed, ambitious programs of economic development. Inflation, unemployment, and poverty grew dramatically in already poor Latin American nations. Latin American governments and businesses, reeling under the impact of the recession, found themselves unable to repay high interest loans to hundreds of international banks—thereby threatening the solvency of these banks and the entire international credit system. The dreams of the reformers of the 1960s who argued that Latin America would develop with rapid industrialization, fast-growing cities, and agrarian reform programs disappeared in the economic stagnation and setbacks of the late 1970s and 1980s. Industrial growth had not provided enough good paying jobs or brought Latin America economic independence. Fast-growing cities more and more became places of fast-growing slums. Finally, agrarian reform programs turned out to be virtually worthless because governments failed to redistribute land in behalf of landless or land-poor Latin American peasants.

Despite all these setbacks and failures, the Latin American people did not seem discouraged. They continued to struggle to raise themselves out of poverty and military dictatorship.

Hundreds of thousands of demonstrators and strikers opposed dictatorships in Argentina, Chile, and Uruguay in the early 1980s. In 1983, the Argentine military dictatorship fell, and the Argentine people elected a new civilian government. Brazil, though seemingly controlled by its armed forces, never had so many independent worker and peasant unions or professional groups and newspapers defending the causes of democracy, better health and education systems, more jobs, and greater economic equality. In most of Latin America, the Catholic Church had taken a stand in favor of social justice and democracy and against continuing poverty and dictatorship.

These themes dominate the discussion of Latin America offered in this volume. The book is largely the result of six extended visits to Latin America during the last ten years. Its perspective was acquired in talking with or listening to Latin Americans and especially in reading what Latin Americans write about their past and present.

1

LATIN AMERICA:
ITS LAND AND PEOPLE

The 375 million people of Latin America live in twenty-five countries. They make up ten percent of the world's population and possess about fifteen percent of its land. They do not occupy this land in equally distributed numbers. Few areas of the world are so unevenly settled and developed. Vast stretches, especially the Amazon basin in the center of South America, remain virtually uninhabited. The people of Latin America have always preferred to gather in clusters rather than to spread out. Much land remains open today for frontier settlement.

VARIED LANDSCAPE

The region's geography is one explanation for this remarkable pattern of settlement. The Latin American landscape is dramatic and varied. A satellite passing over the area from Mexico in the north to Argentina and Chile in the south would transmit a picture of mountains, plains, rivers, islands, and mainland. A closer view would reveal such important details as tropical rain forests; dry, inhospitable deserts; green, fertile mountain valleys; gently rolling upland regions; and well-watered plains.

Scanning northern Mexico, the satellite would show a wide, dry plateau bracketed with mountain ranges. These ranges seem to merge into a single, rugged mountainous

PLATEAU

RAIN FOREST

DESERT

MOUNTAINS

The uneven settlement of Latin America has been partly due to varied extremes of climate and terrain.

area as the land itself narrows further south. The bulk of the Mexican people live in this narrowing, rugged land in central and southern Mexico. Mexico City is the core of this densely populated zone.

Moving toward the Isthmus of Panama, a narrow strip of land that connects North and South America, our imaginary satellite would show that the mountain ranges of Mexico continue underwater in an easterly direction toward the Caribbean, where they emerge as the Greater Antilles, a chain of islands. Included in this island chain are such nations as Cuba, Jamaica, Haiti, and the Dominican Republic. Puerto Rico, a possession of the United States, is also part of the Greater Antilles.

While spinning south, the satellite passes over Central America. The viewer will notice that all of the Central American republics have mountains or highlands and that Mexico has become a wet zone, generously supplied with rainfall. Reaching the continent of South America, the satellite sends back a kaleidoscopic view. Perhaps the most dramatic feature is the high, jagged mountain range that spreads along the entire west coast of South America. Beginning as a "Y" formation around oil-rich Lake Maracaibo in Venezuela, the Andes march south over four thousand miles in three parallel chains. The combined average width of these mountains ranges from two hundred to four hundred miles. They are at their highest and widest in Bolivia. Bolivia's most important city, La Paz, lies nestled in a valley that is 12,500 feet above sea level. The majority of the people of all the west coast countries of South America, with the exception of Chile, live clustered in the high valleys of the Andes.

East of the Andes a variety of features appear. In the north and east are the Guiana highlands and the flat *llanos*. These llanos, found mostly in Venezuela, are two hundred miles wide and six hundred miles long and are one of Latin America's two spacious plains. They have been used for cattle ranching rather than for farming. The reasons are easy to understand. Six months a year, the llanos are hot and wet. The other six months, they are hot and dry. The soil is often poor quality clay. Flood control projects, irrigation works, and an attack on the great variety of mosquitoes, flies, and other insects that thrive in the llanos are necessary to turn these plains into a large-scale supplier of meat and grains. The Venezuelan government has been slowly introducing these changes.

To the south of the llanos is a geographic complex that dwarfs any other in Latin America, except the Andes. It is the huge Amazon basin, which occupies nearly one-half of South America and includes the world's largest tropical rain forest. For the most part, the Amazon basin is in Brazil, but thousands of square miles of it extend into Venezuela, eastern Colombia, Ecuador, Peru, and Bolivia. Flowing through it is the Amazon River and its tributaries. Together, they constitute the world's mightiest river system. This system drains forty percent of the land area of South America.

During its course, the Amazon sometimes attains a width of three miles. It carries at least five times more water to the ocean than its nearest competitor, the Mississippi. The water of the Amazon flows into the Atlantic with such force that one can find fresh water for two hundred miles into the ocean. The Amazon basin, however, has only begun to be penetrated. Most of its resources must still be discovered and inventoried.

Our hypothetical satellite is now speeding over the southern half of South America. Here, the continent narrows. Three outstanding land features are evident. In Brazil, south of the Amazon, there is a great mass of highlands. For nearly two thousand miles along the coast, these highlands practically rise out of the Atlantic Ocean like a wall. Little or no coastal plain exists over this lengthy stretch. This abrupt wall is called the *Great Escarpment.*

The remarkable feature about the Brazilian highlands is

that they reach their greatest height at their coastal beginnings. Thereafter, they slowly descend and move into the interior, falling away and down from the Great Escarpment. This fact explains why many rivers that begin in the seven thousand to eight thousand feet heights only a few miles from the coast wind their way hundreds of miles inland. Much of the Brazilian highlands remains a frontier area. Generations of Brazilian leaders have hoped that the interior would be settled; but full settlement is still just a hope.

Moving farther south over the rapidly narrowing continent, a sparsely settled lowland interior plain in Paraguay and northern Argentina called the *Gran Chaco* comes into view. An area of tall grass, interrupted by scrub forest, the Gran Chaco was the scene of a gruesome war between Paraguay and Bolivia from 1932 to 1938. The war was fought for possession of lands that, according to rumor, were rich in oil. History has partially confirmed these suspicions. Eventually, oil was discovered—but in the adjacent Argentine *Chaco*, and not the land over which Paraguay and Bolivia fought.

To the east and south of the Gran Chaco, around the mouth of the Río de la Plata system, lies the *Pampa,* one of the most generously endowed of the world's plains. The rich soil of the pampa has made Argentines and Uruguayans among the world's best-fed people.

Flowing from Paraguay and Brazil through northern Argentina and into a muddy estuary is the Río de la Plata river system. This system can accommodate ocean-going vessels one thousand miles upstream to Asunción, the capital of Paraguay. The main branch of the Río de la Plata system, the Paraná-Paraguay River, is the most heavily used natural artery of commerce in all of Latin America.

This rapid view of Latin America's physical geography should confirm that the area is anything but uniform and that it is often uninviting to settlement. However, the barriers posed by Latin America's often unfavorable geography must not be overrated. Shallow, silt-laden harbors can be dredged and made suitable for the deepest ocean-going vessels, as it has at Buenos Aires, Argentina, one of the world's great port cities. Highways can and have been constructed through the earthquake-ridden Andes, even though they are twisting, narrow, two-lane roads that follow an unending series of hairpin curves, and force cars and trucks to creep along in second gear. During the 1970s, the Brazilian government constructed a road through the Amazon rain forest because the government wanted to connect Brazil's poverty-ridden, drought-stricken northeast with the unpopulated Amazon wilderness. This highway cuts through hundreds of miles of dense rain forest, crosses periodically flooded grasslands, and fords mile-wide rivers. It stretches all the way to the border with Peru.

The more than 800 thousand miles of roads (only ninety thousand of which are all-weather) and the eighty-five thousand miles of railroads attest to the fact that the rugged geography of Latin America is not an insurmountable obstacle. Furthermore, the airplane has linked places and areas that roads, railways, and rivers have not been able to bring together. Cargo-carrying planes have been especially important. The small, level clearing needed for takeoff and landing can be built for a small fraction of the cost and time required by the railroad and highway. Many areas of Latin America would remain isolated today and deprived of larger regional and national markets were it not for the arrival and departure of freight-carrying airplanes.

As important as geography has been, it is not the element that best explains what is now happening or has happened in Latin America. For example, whatever potential wealth was known to exist, geography has rarely been a barrier to getting at it. Nothing in Latin American history has been more certain than the mining of valuable natural resources by cheap labor, no matter how inaccessible or forbidding the location. The towering Andes mountains, rich in silver, the bone dry Atacama Desert of northern Chile with its copper mines, and, presently, the Amazon rain forest with its reserves of different metal and minerals have not posed, nor will they in the future pose, barriers to human settlement or to large scale industrial production.

Developing wealth by means of cheap or forced labor has probably been the most important continuing process in Latin American history. This process, in turn, is responsible for the riches and poverty seen everywhere in the region.

THE PEOPLE

The Latin American people have come principally from three areas of the world. The American Indian, native to the region, may have originally numbered anywhere from thirteen to fifty million. These peoples were densely settled in the islands of the Caribbean; in the highlands, mountains, and Yucatán peninsula of Central America; and in the Andes Mountains of South America. In other areas, the Indian population was more sparse. There were probably no more than a million and a half Indians in all of Brazil. By comparison, some of the islands of the Caribbean may have had as many people as all of Brazil.

From Africa came fifteen million human beings destined for a life of slavery. Slaves were most highly concentrated in Brazil and the Caribbean Islands. However, at least a few black slaves—and sometimes quite a few—were worked in nearly all parts of Latin America.

From Europe came nearly fifteen million people. Their migration has continued from 1492 to the present time. Indeed, the majority of them have arrived since 1870.

In addition to these three main groups, a few hundred thousand Asians migrated to Latin America. Settlers from India have come to the former British colonies of Jamaica and Guyana. Nearly 250 thousand Japanese settled in

Brazil. Small groups of Chinese emigrated to Peru and Brazil.

The Indian, the African, the European, and combinations of these three groups of people make up the overwhelming majority of today's Latin American population. Over the centuries, they have intermingled culturally and biologically in a "melting pot" that dwarfs anything known in the United States.

In the beginning, great gaps separated the three groups. Race and personal status were interlinked. The European came as a conqueror, ruler, and master. The African came as a slave, who labored for the European master class. The Indian occupied a dual status. He was exploited by the European, who demanded free labor, food, and commodities as a tribute. The Indian was also a ward to be protected, Christianized, and re-made into a European peasant.

As soon as the European arrived, the process of miscegenation, or race mixture, began. Out of this process came new individuals who were neither European nor Indian. They were soon joined by the children of African slaves and their European masters. A bewildering variety of unions eventually occurred, and the offspring they produced were given a host of names. The child of an Indian and a European was called a *mestizo*. The union of African and European produced a *mulatto*, and that of the Indian and the African, a *zambo*. Many other names were later added in the effort to distinguish different racial combinations. Given the extent of race mixture in Latin America, such distinctions were impossible to maintain.

Yet, color remains a way of classifying people today. In Brazil's multi-racial society, for example, census takers label people black, brown, yellow, or white. But one Brazilian's definition of "brown" will be "white" or "black" to another Brazilian. Color is a highly subjective idea in Latin America. It lies, quite inconsistently and unpredictably, in the eyes of the beholder.

(United Nations photo/Jerry Frank)

Indians, such as these members of the Cuna tribe of Panama, constitute one of the three major racial groupings in Latin America.

One fact stands out. The individual whose genes contain different combinations from America, Europe, and Africa has become the characteristic Latin American type. The only exceptions among the Spanish-speaking republics are Costa Rica, Uruguay, and Argentina, whose populations are almost exclusively of European origin. Haiti, on the other hand, is an almost exclusively black republic.

Race mixture itself cannot be thought of scientifically as either a good or bad process. Some Latin Americans have argued that it was necessary for their nation's past success. They also imply that it will strengthen them in the future. In some places, then—most notably in Brazil and Mexico—race mixture is thought of as being positive.

Race mixture is one of the long-term processes of Latin American history. It is necessary to examine this history, which may be conveniently broken into three periods: the colonial period, lasting about three hundred years (1492-1790); the independence period, lasting approximately thirty-five years (1790-1825); and the period since independence (1825 to the present), especially the years since 1930.

2

THE COLONIAL PERIOD

INDIANS, AFRICANS, AND EUROPEANS MAKE THEIR MARK

The most dramatic events of the colonial period occurred at the beginning when a few hundred Spaniards and Portuguese conquered millions of Indians and then subjected them to an alien colonial rule.

The conquest is all the more striking because of its relative ease. Only a few Indian people were able to withstand the initial Spanish and Portuguese assaults. The Mayans held out in the Yucatán peninsula for a quarter of a century. Indian warfare flickered on the Brazilian frontier for a few decades. Only the Araucanians in Chile and certain plains Indians in Argentina were able to remain independent during the entire colonial period. But they were forced to retreat to remote areas of southern Chile and Argentina, which Europeans found either undesirable or too difficult to conquer.

The millions of New World Indians varied as much in their cultures and achievements as any people could. They spoke hundreds of languages and organized themselves into a great variety of social units. Some went nude and lived together in villages of longhouses. Indians such as these greeted the Portuguese when they arrived on the shores of Brazil in 1500. Others wore woven cotton clothing and lived in solidly constructed brick houses in great cities, as did the Aztecs and other Indian peoples of Central America. The Incas built a great empire, which included millions of people spread over the modern-day countries of Ecuador, Peru, and Bolivia and which extended even into parts of Argentina and Chile. Although a few primitive Indians obtained food only through hunting and gathering, the vast majority had mastered the techniques of agriculture.

THE ACHIEVEMENT OF INDIAN AGRICULTURE

The degree to which the Latin American Indians mastered agriculture varied. The Tupinamba, who occupied the coast of Brazil, farmed in a way that quickly exhausted the soil. These hard-working people had to clear away the trees of the dense coastal forest. During the dry season, they would cut the trees at the base of their trunks. The fallen debris would then be burned. Having cleared the ground of all but the tree trunks, they planted manioc, a vegetable that grows underground. When harvested, the manioc tuber is as large as a medium-sized squash. When processed, it yields a flour that has the highest starch content of any known staple crop. The Tupinamba usually harvested two crops of manioc a year. After two or three years of this kind of agriculture, the soil was exhausted. Declining yields forced the Indians to abandon their villages and search for new lands. The Portuguese settlers in Brazil adopted this rather wasteful form of agriculture. Like the hammock and bathing, it was one of several cultural practices they borrowed from the Tupinamba.

In several of the islands of the Caribbean, the native Arawak population heaped freshly cleared land into knee-high mounds several feet in diameter. In the loose soil of these mounds they planted manioc, sweet potatoes, beans, squash, and even corn. Water was usually plentiful, but where the land was dry, they dug irrigation ditches to bring water from nearby streams. The Arawaks also used a variety of fishing techniques and implements. These included the hook and line, a primitive harpoon, nets, and even drugs that

(United Nations photo)

The cultivation of sugar cane was part of an agricultural system that was imposed by the colonial powers.

stupefied the fish. Pigeons, doves, parrots, and a rabbit-like animal were hunted and eaten. There was enough food to support a native island population that numbered in the millions.

Within fifty years of the arrival of the Europeans, not only was this highly productive Arawak Caribbean agriculture completely disorganized, but the native population itself was exterminated. The Indians of the Caribbean died by the millions, chiefly victims of European diseases, of which smallpox was the most deadly.

Meanwhile, on the mainland in Mexico, the mighty Aztecs were growing corn, as did all the Indian peoples of Middle America. In Mexico, land was a scarce resource that needed to be carefully used. Corn was therefore raised in fields that periodically lay uncultivated to avoid soil exhaustion. Canals were dug to irrigate dry land. To prevent soil erosion, the Aztecs prohibited destruction of forests, a policy their Spanish conquerors unfortunately did not follow. Like the Arawaks, the Aztecs devised an imaginative method of intensive agriculture. Large, oval-shaped wicker baskets were made and anchored to the shallow bottom of the lake waters that surrounded the Aztec capital of Tenochtitlán. These baskets were then filled with earth and planted with crops. In this way, more productive land was created. This lake agriculture is the source of the famous floating gardens of Xochimilco.

The Aztec culture of Mexico, while impressive, was not so highly developed as that of the Incas in South America. Here in the dry Andes, the Incas terraced the steep mountain slopes. A particular terrace would have a hundred or more steps on which potatoes, squash, beans, and corn were cultivated. Water was hoarded in reservoirs built at the top of the terraced flight of steps. Masters of irrigation techniques, knowing precisely how much water should be released at a given time, the Incas were able to water each terrace step, flooding none, leaving none dry. The Incas also used the excrement of llamas and birds to fertilize their fields. Taken together, the Indian peoples of Latin America may be conveniently divided into three groups: First, there were the hunting and gathering peoples who usually knew no fixed place of settlement and whose technology was almost nonexistent. Second, there were agricultural peoples who lived in permanent or semi-permanent villages and who supplemented their crop-grown diet by hunting, fishing, and gathering. Finally, there were the civilizations of Middle America (Aztec and Mayan) and South America (Incan) whose achievements in agriculture, crafts, government and city planning, architecture, and engineering amazed their Spanish conquerors and still impress observers today.

The Europeans Confront the Indian

The stunning achievements of the Indian civilizations deeply impressed the Spaniards. Many Spaniards and Portuguese were also initially struck by the apparent innocence of the more primitive Indians. Here were people so free of shame that they went about completely unclothed. They worked hard cultivating their fields, did not engage in wars for empire, did not crave gold except for personal ornamentation, and lived in a world that remained green and fruitful throughout the year. The first Europeans wondered aloud whether the New World might be the lost paradise of Adam and Eve. Columbus himself at one time thought that Venezuela's Orinoco River was the river of Paradise and that a journey upstream would probably lead to the rediscovery of the long-lost Garden of Eden.

The achievements of the Aztec, Mayan, and Incan civilizations fascinated the newcomers. However, neither the innocence nor the magnificent civilizations of the Indians spared them from destruction. The Spanish *conquistador*, as his name implies, came to conquer. The Portuguese came first to carry off brazilwood for use in preparing dyes. Then, when no other quick, easy wealth was discovered, the Portuguese established sugar plantations, first using Indian and, later, African slave labor.

THE AFRICAN CONTRIBUTION
TO THE NEW WORLD

The African people came from widely scattered areas of their native continent. Like the Indians, they spoke hundreds of different languages and held a great variety of beliefs and values. Africans had also mastered superior techniques of agriculture. They cultivated their fields with their own type of short-handled hoe. In well-organized societies of West Africa, the men did the heavy work of clearing the fields and preparing them for planting. The women tended and harvested the crops. The produce was sold in busy markets. Africans were hard-working, well-disciplined farming people who possessed superior methods of growing and distributing food.

The African achievements were important in Latin American history. Because Africans excelled in agriculture and because they were sturdy, disciplined workers, they became highly desired as plantation workers.

The African forced to migrate to the New World was admirably equipped for a variety of tasks. He was a master craftsman, with knowledge of smelting and ironworking. Unlike the Indian, he was able to survive European diseases. The African was highly adaptable. Just as he had mastered most of the important techniques of civilization in Africa, so he was able to perform any task that the ruling European group of the New World asked him to perform. In Brazil, he was a productive farmer, plantation laborer, and miner. He could cook and make clothing. He was a blacksmith and ironworker. He was a courageous soldier. Black slaves were often the principal companions of the master, his wife, and children. No important economic activity could have taken place in colonial Brazil without the African. A prominent white Brazilian writing in the 1880s affirmed that it was the African slave, rather than the European freeman, who civilized Brazil.

No one of the cultures—European, Indian, or African—was markedly superior or able to overwhelm the other two. The three groups interacted in the New World of Latin America. They borrowed heavily from one another and contributed to one another. Nevertheless, a special word needs to be said about the ruling Europeans.

Throughout the colonial period, Europeans effectively exercised power. Europeans controlled governments. Europeans made and enforced laws. The New World of Latin America was conquered first by the Spaniards and Portuguese and later by the French, English, and Dutch. Neither the Indian nor the African was able to challenge seriously Spanish and Portuguese rule during the colonial period. It is true that black slaves and oppressed Indians frequently rebelled against the European master class. It is also true that these rebellions did not succeed in the long run. Europeans brought with them a remarkable capacity to rule and dominate others. They also brought the determination to exploit the people and resources of Latin America.

EXPLOITATION DURING THE COLONIAL PERIOD

According to one dictionary, "exploit" may have three meanings: to make use of, utilize, turn to account; to turn selfishly or unfairly to one's own account; or to make profit from the labor of others. In Latin American history, all three forms of exploitation have been widely practiced. Indian and African labor was used for the profit of various individuals within Latin America. Precious metals mined in the New World were used to pay the debts of over-extended Spanish and Portuguese monarchs. These same metals came to serve as money and credit, stimulating European commerce and industry.

Perhaps the first and most famous acts of exploitation were those of the Spanish conquerors or conquistadores. As a reward for subjugating Indians, *some* conquistadores demanded the right to collect Indian tribute. The Spanish government responded by establishing a remarkable institution called *encomienda*, which is derived from the Spanish verb *encomendar* meaning "to entrust." The idea was to entrust a number of Indians to a conquistador who would be responsible for instructing them in the Christian faith and the ways of Spanish civilization. In return, the thankful Indian was to pay tribute. Tribute was supposed to take the form of commodities such as food and clothing. But hard labor and personal service were also rendered.

The encomienda quickly became an institution of exploitation. Indignant voices, mostly clergymen's, denounced the system as a form of disguised slavery that was destroying the Indian population.

In the early 1540s, the Spanish king, Charles V, listened to these critical voices. He approved a code of New Laws (1542) that attacked the worst encomienda abuses. One of the New Laws even looked forward to the abolition of the encomienda system altogether. It stated that when the current holder of a grant of Indians in encomienda died, the grant would die with him. The Indians would have a new status. They would be direct subjects of the king.

The New Laws could not be enforced. The conquistadores prepared to revolt. They claimed that they could not live without encomienda tribute. Some clergymen and religious orders joined them. They argued that Indians held in encomienda were more likely to be converted to Christianity and that their tribute was essential to the support of the Church. When a Spanish viceroy tried to enforce the New Laws in Peru, he was met with armed resistance. A civil war erupted. The unfortunate viceroy was captured by rebellious conquistadores and beheaded.

The New Laws of the King of Spain were clearly unacceptable. Charles V, therefore, repealed the most important ones. To enforce them was to risk a permanent rebellion by the conquistador class and, perhaps, the loss of the most valuable part of the New World empire.

The evils of encomienda continued. There were other types of exploitation as well. The Indians of Peru were subjected to the *mita*, a system of forced public labor taken over from the Incas. Under the Incas, subject Indian peoples owed a tax that was paid by work on public projects. Individual villages had to provide a number of able-bodied men to work on the royal highways or to build the narrow, swaying, braided vine bridges that crossed the deep canyons of the Andes. They had to build and maintain highway inns, which provided refuge for travelers. The idea behind the mita or labor tax was to provide indispensable public service.

The Spaniards adopted the mita to their own purposes. Indians were put to work constructing roads and public buildings. They were also sent to work in the mines. Everyone in Spain believed that gold and silver were necessary to make Spain powerful and respected. Therefore, Indians were forced to work in the mines.

The king's councilors were quick to decree laws that limited hours and provided wages for Indians forced to work in mines under the mita system. Like the New Laws for encomienda, these decrees could not be enforced. For example, Indians were sometimes compelled to work in the mines for twenty-four hours straight, even when the king's laws said that they were to work in eight-hour shifts.

Working conditions were frightful. The Indian descended into the deep mines on loose, thong stepladders, often rotted with age. A simple pick and shovel were used to loosen the precious ore. It was then loaded into sacks whose total weight would reach perhaps fifty pounds. Burdened with this sack, the Indian would make the dangerous climb to the surface.

His food was a small portion of dry corn; the traditional Inca beverage, chicha; and coco leaves. These coco leaves, when chewed, would release a narcotic that dulled the pain of cold and hunger. What did the Indian do with the hard-earned wages that the king's law said he must be paid? He was lucky to receive even a part of them. The mining operator made a deduction for food, chicha, and coco. He was also permitted to deduct a fine if the Indian failed to deliver his assigned quota of ore. More of the wages were deducted as tribute owed to the king. The Indian was left with little or nothing for his enforced labor. Sometimes he was even left in debt.

It is important to note that the different kinds of exploitation that were common occurrences in the colonial period did not end when independence arrived. Before the great Bolivian revolution of 1952, groups of Indians in this predominantly Indian country were still forced to perform mita labor services. A revolution was needed before this practice could be stopped.

THE HACIENDA AND FAZENDA

An even more remarkable institution of exploitation that has survived the centuries is the *hacienda*, or as it is called in Brazil, the *fazenda*. The hacienda or fazenda is the name for a large land unit in Latin America. Established during the colonial period, this institution survived the wars of independence and even grew in importance during the nineteenth century. One authority has written that for a hundred years, from 1820 to 1920, the hacienda set the tone and determined the quality of Latin American culture. We can say with only slight exaggeration that before 1920 Latin America was a big farm.

Until the middle of the twentieth century, the vast majority of Latin Americans were rural people. Land was of critical importance. To own a piece of land was to have enough to eat and a means of earning a living. Indian villages built their life around the cultivation of traditional lands. The loss of these traditional lands meant the death of the village. Land guaranteed survival and a customary way of life to the peasant and the ordinary Indian villager. Any government that attempted to take land away from either group was asking for revolution and civil war.

Land also conferred status. In the rural countries of Latin America, anyone or any group that owned land automatically had some independence and importance. The few individuals and families who owned large pieces of land enjoyed great importance in the community, as well as great wealth and power.

The owners of large landholdings are usually called *hacendados* in Spanish-speaking Latin America and *fazendeiros* in Portuguese-speaking Brazil. Their status, wealth, and power did not come simply from owning the land. The hacendado or fazendeiro virtually owned the people who worked on his land. He was, therefore, not only a landowner but a person who controlled the lives of others. He dominated the lives of his tenants, or *peons*, who lived in a state of submissiveness.

To understand how this state of affairs came to exist, we must return to the colonial period. At that time, individuals received title to large tracts of land in both Portuguese Brazil and Spanish America. But this land had little value in and of itself. People were needed to settle on it and to cultivate it.

Having acquired the land, the landowner was forced to find ways of getting people to work it. In some places, the solution was simple. He bought slaves. In most of Spanish America, it was more common for the landowner to allow and even to invite Indians or other free rural people to settle on his land. He would turn over to them some of the poorer lands. Often they were dry patches of soil far from a source of water, or they might be on a steep hillside or even a mountain slope. In addition, the hacendado might provide a simple house for his peon.

The peon who accepted these questionable gifts was required to work for the hacendado. Usually he would have to work a given amount of time on the land the owner reserved for himself. This was the best land, and on it was raised a crop such as corn, which could be sold for cash in the market of a nearby town. In addition, the peon would be asked to construct and repair the hacienda buildings. These might be the owner's house, his barns and stables, or even his chapel. A chapel was usually on the property because the hacienda was large enough and the people who lived on it numerous enough to make a congregation of worshippers. The owner often believed that he had an obligation to provide his own family and his peons with a place of worship. Here we have another important feature of the hacienda: It was almost a complete world in itself, and nearly succeeded in being a self-sufficient unit. It provided its own food and housing. It had its own religious center. It had its own fiestas. It even had its own store, or *tienda de raya*, where clothing, seed, tools, and liquor could be purchased.

From the preceding description, it may not seem that the hacienda was necessarily an exploitative or unjust institution. After all, the tenant received a home, a piece of land, and easy access to virtually every necessity. In return, he had only to labor a certain number of days for the owner.

A closer examination will reveal some other facts. The peon's or tenant's home was most likely a shack or hovel barely fit for human habitation. The hacendado, meanwhile, lived in a spacious house filled with a large number of servants. These servants were not paid. Providing them was one more of the peon's obligations. The servants were seen but seldom heard. They were meek and obedient and showed in another way the hacendado's great prestige and social status. The tienda de raya may have been a conveniently located store, but it was one where the local peons ran up debts. They were never able to pay these debts. After a peon's death, these obligations were inherited by the next generation. Such debts were used to restrain the freedom of movement of the peons who dared not leave the estate until they had paid what they owed.

Defenders of the hacienda might say that the hacendado looked upon his tenants as children whom he had to protect in a fatherly way. But he was a stern father. The hacendado, for example, often sponsored a wedding involving his tenants. However, the wedding could not have occurred in the first place without the hacendado's permission. The hacendado and his wife also served as godparents to the peon's children. Godparenthood or *compadrazgo* was widespread in Latin America and carried important responsibilities. Godchildren and their families had to be aided in times of distress, whether such distress was illness, the failure of a crop, or some other difficulty. But peons who received such paternalistic aid and comfort had to be absolutely loyal and obedient to the owner. Should the peon display independence or oppose the hacendado's wishes, he risked expulsion or other forms of punishment, such as whipping. The whipping post was a fixture on many haciendas. Disrespectful, disobedient peons were tied to it and whipped, as the owner impressed upon them and everyone else in his "family" that his wishes were law. In some places, when seeking new employment, a tenant was required to show a document signed by the hacendado giving him permission to leave his estate.

In Latin America, the relationship between the wealthy landowner and his tenant families has been one of more than mutual convenience. It has been a social relationship without equality—a relationship in which the dominance of the hacendado was in striking contrast to the submissiveness of the peon. It has been a relationship in which the hacendado took his wealth and status for granted, while the peon had little hope of improving his position.

The Hacienda as an Economic Unit

It is not simply the hacienda's social relationships that have made it the object of criticism. There is also the question of its failure to make proper use of its lands. Critics not only charge that the hacienda has oppressed and humiliated its lowly peon tenants but that it has also failed to use its lands efficiently for food production. The hacienda, therefore, has become the target of those who want social justice for rural people and enough food for a nation's growing population—especially its city population.

Of course, the hacienda did not originate for the purpose of producing as much food as possible. In the past, local markets were usually too small to absorb large harvests. The hacendado purposely limited the size of his cash crop. If he grew too much food, the market would be glutted and prices would fall. He held down production to keep the price reasonably high.

The lack of roads and rapid transportation meant that the hacienda could not sell in the larger, distant urban market. A long trip raised the price and might have spoiled the food. The hacendado became accustomed to selling in the local market, where a little food was often enough. He had no incentive to make the best possible use of his lands. If the primitive wood plow and unfertilized semi-arid soil produced enough for the local market, he was satisfied.

Even today, with a growing network of roads and reduced costs of transportation, the hacienda and fazenda often continue to be underproductive. The owner is satisfied with the income he receives when half the output of his land is simply transferred to him by unpaid peons. Furthermore, the low income of millions of Latin Americans does not allow them to buy the food they need at a price that will satisfy the landowner.

If the hacendado or fazendeiro were to invest heavily in modern farm equipment or pay salaries to farm workers, his production would rise, but his costs would also rise. The food would be too expensive for the badly-paid Latin Americans who make up the majority of the population. Food production remains low because tens of millions of Latin Americans do not earn enough Mexican *pesos*, Brazilian *cruzeiros*, or Peruvian *soles*. Millions of Latin Americans continue to be undernourished. The hacienda and fazenda, created during the colonial period and the nineteenth century, also continues.

√THE COLONIAL POLITICAL SYSTEM

The Spanish and Portuguese empires were established at a time when kings ruled the states of Europe. It is not surprising that political power in Latin America was organized so that the king or his royal officials exercised nearly all of it. In the New World, the highest of these officials were called viceroys or vice-kings. Their tasks were to execute the laws of the king, to protect the New World empire from foreign attack, and to raise revenues. The last matter was especially important, since the ruling monarchs were usually short of money and had great difficulty paying for their European wars.

There were many other royal officials who helped to carry out the orders of the king. Churchmen could be relied upon to back the king's policies. The Church, by preaching obedience to the monarch and praising his goodness, provided strong support in the distant New World empire.

Perhaps the most important point to remember is that law and authority came from the king or his officials and not from the people or their representatives. There were no legislatures or important elected bodies in the New World. During the colonial period, Latin America did not have representative institutions. Groups or individuals who had complaints or desired new laws addressed themselves to the king or his officials.

Today in Latin America, governments continue this

(United Nations photo)

The Catholic Church has been an influential institution throughout the
development of Latin America.

tradition by having powerful chief executives. Only one country, Uruguay, tried for a time to do without a single, strong chief executive. Latin American dictators and freely elected presidents have often been given almost kingly powers. Colombia and Chile are almost the only Latin American countries where regularly elected legislatures have played important roles over a long period of time. The Chilean legislature was once strong enough to remove a president. The president resisted, and a brief civil war followed. After he had been defeated by the forces of the legislature, the humiliated ex-president, José Manuel Balmaceda, committed suicide. These events occurred in 1891.

The Chilean legislature, or Parliament, continued to have great power and importance until 1973 when a military revolt ended more than a century of free elections and representative democracy in Chile. A military dictatorship replaced one of Latin America's oldest democracies.

⋎RELIGION

The Catholic Church has always been important in Latin America. During the colonial period, it was an essential element in society and a pillar of the king's authority. Churchmen arrived with the European conquest. From the beginning, the monarchs of Spain and Portugal were concerned with "winning" the souls of Indians for Christianity. Missionary work and conversion were theoretically as important as winning an empire and discovering riches. Churchmen came with conquerors, traders, royal officials, personal servants, and adventurers.

At first, these churchmen tended to be members of religious orders. They were Franciscans, Dominicans, and Jesuits. Later, when their work of conversion was presumably finished, secular clergymen—not members of religious orders—took over Church government and filled the majority of its offices, from parish priest to archbishop. The royal government passed on appointments of churchmen and collected Church revenues. In these ways, there was a close, unbreakable tie between Church and state.

As the colonial period unfolded, the Church became a great landowner. Finally, it was the wealthiest of all institutions. In colonial Mexico, it was said, a will that did not include a bequest to the Church was taken as an act against religion. In 1810, on the eve of independence, the Church in Mexico either owned outright or held mortgages on eighty percent of all privately controlled land.

Such wealth eventually became a costly burden. Because the Church was powerful and wealthy, it was often blamed for the troubles of a particular society. Today, the Church has lost most of its land and wealth. Freed of great riches, it can more comfortably exercise spiritual responsibilities.

Catholicism has been one of the major unifying forces in Latin America. With regional and class conflicts strong in many individual Latin American countries, Catholicism was able to help bind nations together. During the colonial period, a strong Church worked in tandem with a strong state. After independence, a still-strong Church was frequently in a position either to support or oppose a weak, central government. As time passed, governments have recovered their authority and Latin American societies have become more worldly. But the Church is still influential. Pastoral letters of high churchmen can still play crucial roles in bolstering or overthrowing a government. A churchman who joins a guerrilla movement or speaks out against a dictatorship performs a dramatic act that may rivet public attention and contribute to political upheaval.

A final important word needs to be added about religion. One of the most remarkable facts of Latin American history is that Catholic Christianity, despite its position as the official religion, did not eliminate all competing religions. Both the African and the Indian, although they adopted much of Christianity, continued to follow many of their own non-Christian religious practices. In the Caribbean and Brazil, drums continue to sound rhythmically, invoking African deities. *Vodun* in Haiti, *Santeria* in Cuba, and *Candomble, Macumba,* and *Chango* in Brazil are a few of the names given to these popular and compelling Afro-American religious rites. Recent evidence indicates that their followers are growing, rather than diminishing, in many places. They are certainly growing in many Brazilian cities, where these rites give the impression of being the most vital of all religions.

Another example of Latin America's multi-religious heritage may be drawn from a Mayan Indian village in nineteenth century Guatemala. In the center of the village is a Christian cross dedicated to the local patron saint. An annual festival honoring the saint will take place. The saint's help is believed to be necessary to secure protection for village and crops. The festival will include ritualistic drinking of *aguardiente*, a Mayan tradition which preceded the conquest. Villagers will dance the steps of the *Vasqueria* and *Jarana* to music played on the violin and the horn. Both the dances and the musical instruments were brought from Spain. After a while the atmosphere will change. The women will be banished. The traditional Spanish dances and European instruments will be set aside. Men will appear in masks wearing feathered headdresses and crowns. The wood gong, turtle shell rattle, and clay flute—all ancient Mayan instruments—now provide the musical background as the serious business of winning the patron saint's protection continues.

✗ RACE AND SOCIAL STANDING

The relationship between race and social standing is rather complicated. We already know what racial groups were present in Latin America. We also know that race mixture and the mixing of different cultural characteristics have occurred on a massive scale throughout Latin American history.

Originally, such mixing and blending were not supposed to occur. The monarchs of Spain and Portugal tried to keep the three racial groups of Europeans, Indians, and Africans separated. They were segregated in different ways. Blacks and whites sat in different parts of the churches in colonial Brazil. Again in colonial Brazil, separate religious brotherhoods existed for blacks and whites. There were separate military units. Indians in the Spanish empire were supposed to live by themselves in villages. Except for royal officials and perhaps a priest, Europeans were excluded from these villages.

The state had a policy preventing people of different racial and cultural backgrounds from marrying or living together. Those who entered unapproved marital unions and their children were made to suffer. For example, an Indian who married a mestizo or black was likely to see the children of this marriage deprived of their rights in the Indian village, often including the right to live there. Marriage outside one's own group was proper grounds for disinheritance. In Brazil, black officers were deprived of their commissions in militia units for marrying white women. For a while in the sixteenth century, the King of Spain would not even allow mestizos to enter the priesthood.

In many places, mestizos, mulattos, and black subjects of the king were not permitted to enter universities or to bring a suit in court against white subjects. In the Spanish empire, Indians, mestizos, mulattos, and blacks were not supposed to carry guns or ride horses. Obviously, the state looked upon these groups as potential rebels. Carrying a sword or riding a horse was a privilege of the nobility, a rank from which non-Europeans were almost always excluded.

The Spanish and Portuguese New World empires were full of social rankings. The whites ranked highest, followed by Indians, mestizos, mulattos, free blacks, and finally slaves. The higher a person's rank, the more rights he had and the fewer restrictions he suffered. The Spaniard or Portuguese suffered almost no restrictions except those of marrying beneath his rank or engaging in manual labor, deemed suitable only for slaves or peasants. The slave, on the other hand, had almost no rights. Only with great difficulty could a person move from one group to another, and individuals of low status who behaved like individuals of higher rank might be punished. For example, the right to wear the luxury fabric of silk was reserved for Spaniards. In 1685, the Viceroy of Peru forbid black and mulatto women to wear silk clothing under penalty of having the clothing taken from them. Should they repeat the offense, the penalty was one hundred lashes and expulsion from the city of Lima.

SUMMARY

Let us summarize what we have said about the colonial period. Indians, Europeans, and Africans were brought together in vast numbers. However, they were not treated as equals, and the Europeans were able to dominate the other two peoples. Second, colonial society had many diverse subcultures. The official European civilization was hard pressed to compete with Indian and African cultures. For example, while Roman Catholicism was the only legal religion, Indian and African religious practices flourished, as they do even today. Third, institutions of exploitation and systems of forced labor were widespread. Next, colonial Latin American society consisted of carefully ranked groups. Rank was largely determined by birth and color. Some groups had many privileges while others lacked rights. Finally, political power was monopolized by the king or what we call the executive branch of government.

3

INDEPENDENCE

✓ THE ERA OF INDEPENDENCE

The Latin American independence period lasted about thirty-five years. It began in the early 1790s when the black slaves of Haiti rose up and threw their French masters out of the small island colony. Haiti clung heroically to its independence, which France finally accepted in 1804 after more than ten years of terrible warfare. Haiti was the first Latin American and the second New World nation to win its independence.

The independence period ended in 1824 when Simón Bolívar's patriot army decisively defeated a Spanish royal army at Ayacucho, high in the Andes mountains of Peru. It was a period that saw death, destruction, and civil war devastate some regions. Other areas escaped with little or no destructive conflict.

At the end of the period, most of Latin America was free of foreign rule. Only the islands of the Caribbean, the Guianas on the northeastern coast of South America, and British Honduras in Central America remained colonies. Independent Haiti was the exception in the Caribbean sea of colonies.

✓ TYPES OF INDEPENDENCE MOVEMENTS

There were basically three types of Latin American independence movements: First, there was a true revolutionary upheaval in which the ruling class was violently and totally overthrown and expelled by an uprising of the masses.) This type of movement took place only in Haiti.(Second, there were movements that produced major conflicts and considerable destruction. These wars for independence had the qualities of civil wars as well.)In Venezuela and Mexico, the wars for independence had an additional ingredient of racial conflict.)

In Mexico, the struggle began in 1810 when the white priest, Miguel Hidalgo y Costilla, gathered together an army of sixty thousand Indians and mestizos for the purpose of overthrowing Spanish rule. He asked his followers: "Will you make the effort to recover from the hated Spaniards the lands stolen from your forefathers three hundred years ago?" Their reply was an enthusiastic "yes," judging from the series of victories the army quickly won. But these victories were quickly followed by defeats. The army was poorly equipped, without much discipline, and badly led. Hidalgo himself was captured and executed. His once large army broke into a number of guerrilla bands.

Many Mexican whites must have been relieved when Hidalgo was captured and his army defeated. They had been reluctant to join the priest because they felt his movement would end with the Indian and mestizo taking control of Mexico. Deep differences divided Mexican society. Ever fearful of an Indian and mestizo takeover, most of the whites rallied to the cause of the King of Spain until they were sure that they could win control of Mexico for themselves. When Mexican independence finally came in 1821, the whites did win, but the Indian and mestizo were to have the last word in the colossal Mexican Revolution of 1910-1920.

The third kind of movement for independence was one that achieved independence quickly, easily, and with little or no conflict. Brazil and areas of Central America took this peaceful route to independence. Few changes occurred. Spanish or Portuguese royal officials disappeared. They were replaced by local citizens, usually the representatives of large landowning families. The local landowning class, which had grown rich during the colonial period, now took control of political power.

⅄ THE QUESTION OF SOCIAL REVOLUTIONS

Social revolutions nearly occurred in several Latin American countries during the independence period. A social revolution happens when one class replaces another, wealth is redistributed, and a society's priorities are changed. For example, before a social revolution, a large plantation will be almost entirely given over to the growing of sugar cane for export. Nearly all the income goes to the owner. During a social revolution, the plantation will be taken from the owner. Instead of sugar cane, food crops such as beans, squash, and potatoes will be planted. The harvest will be divided among the workers who have become the new owners. The former owner probably will receive nothing.

In colonial Latin America wealth was monopolized by the large landowners, the merchants, the owners of mines, ruling European officials, and the Church. Haciendas, fazendas, plantations, gold and silver mines, and foreign trade were the most important sources of wealth. Black slaves confined to plantations or semi-enslaved Indians forced to work in mines and textile mills typified the colonial Latin American labor system. People were separated into inferior and superior groups on the basis of color and ethnic origin. A Latin American social revolution would strive to eliminate these systems of property ownership, labor exploitation, and racial injustice.

Until the independence period, the most revolutionary groups were rebellious slaves and Indians. Slave and Indian rebellions during the colonial period point in the direction of authentic Latin American social revolutions. Knowledge of

(United Nations photo/Jerry Frank)

The single crop economies that produce exports, but do not feed the local population, are reflections of the colonial agricultural systems.

these rebellions help us to measure the revolutionary content of later independence movements.

A Slave Rebellion

More than a century before the independence period, tens of thousands of runaway slaves constructed free communities in the northeast of Brazil. These communities received the name of *Palmares*, which refers to their interior location in a palm tree wilderness.

Documents mention the existence of Palmares as early as 1602. Since Palmares was not destroyed until 1695, these communities lasted nearly a century.

The Palmares inhabitants were running from the coastal sugar plantation society. In this society, the plantation owners were the wealthy, dominant class. They owned the sugar plantations and the cane grinding mills. Beneath the owners were a group of tenants who worked the plantations with slave labor. Each tenant owned twenty to fifty slaves. The tenants were required to grind the freshly-cut cane at the owner's mill and to give him half the harvest. The tenant, though himself clearly an exploiter of slave labor, had few rights. The owner could expel him from the plantation. Any improvements made by the tenant then became the property of the owner.

The refined sugar was sent to the port city of Recife. Merchants exported it and imported manufactured and luxury goods. These goods were transferred to the plantation owners, who sometimes owed the merchants large sums of money. The merchants could not easily collect these debts. One who tried was arrested and exiled. The power of the plantation owner was supreme.

Beneath the plantation owners, tenants, and merchants were three other classes. One consisted of poor, landless free people of every color from black to white. Another class consisted of "tamed" Indians who lived in villages organized by Jesuit missionaries. At the base of the society were the slave workers. They made up the largest single group. Indians and especially the free, landless poor often acted as a slave-hunting force. Selling recaptured slaves became an important source of income for poor, free individuals. The slaves themselves ran away from plantation owners who fed them badly, punished them cruelly, and worked them to death. Seven to twelve years was the average working life of a field slave. He was frequently dead by age thirty.

Though poorly fed on the plantations, the runaways discovered in Palmares an abundance of potatoes, corn, beans, manioc, sugar cane, and tobacco. The Palmares communities produced a surplus of food, which was sent to coastal towns in exchange for guns, ammunition, and salt.

Afro-Brazilian culture flourished in Palmares. The fleeing slaves came from different African nations. They overcame their language differences by agreeing to speak Portuguese, the common language they had learned on the plantation. They also created a common Afro-Brazilian religion.

During the seventeenth century, the population of Palmares steadily increased. By 1680, it may have reached thirty thousand. Slaves, Indians, and even free people fled to these interior communities where food was plentiful.

The plantation owners sent military expeditions to destroy the Palmares communities almost every year after 1650. The expeditions were repeatedly defeated or frustrated. Palmares was finally conquered in the middle of the 1690s. The army of destruction was led by a force of slave hunters who travelled hundreds of miles from southern Brazil to participate in the final attack. The victorious slave hunters were allowed to keep the lands and the people they conquered.

Palmares was a glaring challenge to the coastal sugar plantation. Its communities became an agricultural and trading society that produced a surplus of food. In contrast, the plantations produced tons of sugar for export, but little food for its slave workers. Astute, brave leaders were elected chiefs in the Palmares communities. On the coast, a plantation aristocracy exercised power and consulted no one. The Palmares communities broke with slavery, the large estate, and the big landowner. They also broke with the cultivation of a single plantation crop grown for export on the international market. The slaves who ran away to freedom in Palmares had pointed the way to a social and economic revolution.

SOCIAL CHANGE, NOT SOCIAL REVOLUTION

The social revolution toward which Palmares pointed did not take place during the independence period. Except for the successful slave revolt in Haiti, the independence movements were not led by slaves, Indians, or mestizos. Nevertheless, all these different groups participated. Probably one-third of the army of José de San Martin, the liberator of Chile and Peru, was composed of black soldiers. It is not surprising, therefore, that the old colonial system that rigidly classified people according to birth and color was swept away, as were the laws that gave legal privileges to whites while denying them to non-whites. The new Latin American republics wrote constitutions stating that all citizens were equal, regardless of their color. These constitutions no longer permitted the terms "criollo," "mestizo," "mulatto," and "indio" to be used on legal documents. After independence, an individual was legally viewed as a citizen of his country and was not assigned a privileged or underprivileged status according to race or color.

Independence also probably hastened the end of slavery. Some countries—Haiti and Chile, for example—abolished slavery during the era of independence, but it continued in Colombia and Venezuela until 1854. Brazil continued the practice until 1888.

These changes were important, but they did not bring anything approaching individual equality. Latin Americans were as unequal as they had ever been. A small group of large landowners, merchants, mine owners, and foreigners continued to control the wealth and power. The Church continued to be powerful and struggled to keep its lands and privileges. Efforts to deprive the Church of these lands and privileges in nineteenth-century Mexico and Colombia sparked civil wars which brought death to tens of thousands.

The Ideas of the Independence Movements

If the independence movements generally produced social changes rather than a social revolution, they also left what are probably the best set of ideas for nation-building that the Latin American peoples have ever conceived. A summary of these ideas may be found in the *Grito de Dolores*, the battle cry of the Indian and mestizo followers of Father Hildago. "Viva Nuestra Señora de Guadalupe, muera el mal gobierno, mueran los gachupines!" These words mean: "Long live our Lady [i.e., the Virgin] of Guadalupe. Death to the bad government! Death to the Spaniards!"

The appeal to the brown Virgin of Guadalupe recalled that the vast majority of the Mexican population was Indian or mestizo and was deeply religious. Clearly, the new Mexican nation should be constructed around the history, culture, and aspirations of this vast majority.

"Death to the bad government" meant the removal of foreign, Spanish political officials. The new governing class would be Mexican-born.

"Death to the Spaniards" specifically meant the elimination of the hated Spanish merchant class that monopolized trade, housing, the sale of food, and the best jobs in towns and cities. Popular belief held that food prices would fall, that everyone might find a home, and that jobs would be plentiful if this merchant class were eliminated.

The *Grito de Dolores* was one of many independence era statements that offered democratic ideas for Latin American nation building. Clearly, these ideas directed that the new nations should represent the interests of the vast majority and not a small elite of large landowners, mine owners, and merchants. They also required that foreigners should either be excluded from the internal economic and political life of the new nations or allowed to make carefully controlled contributions.

Paraguay Applies Revolutionary Ideas

The *Grito de Dolores* was a Mexican program that failed. Ideas similar to those of the *Grito* appeared elsewhere. Small, weak, half-forgotten Paraguay may have applied these ideas best.

Paraguay is a landlocked country in the center of South America. Surrounding it are Brazil, Bolivia, and Argentina. In the independence period, more than half of the Paraguayan population consisted of Guarani Indians. Even today Paraguay has two official languages: Spanish and Guarani.

The principal Paraguayan independence leader was José Gaspar Rodrigues de Francia. Francia wanted Paraguay to be independent of Spain and all foreign influence. In 1813, while he was president of the *junta* or committee that had led the nation to independence, he ordered all Spaniards to present an inventory of their possessions to government officials. Francia's government then confiscated these possessions and expelled the Spaniards. These Spaniards were rich merchants and former government officials. They were considered foreigners. Without a civil war and in a matter of weeks, Francia forced out of Paraguay the wealthy foreign merchant class.

In 1820, Francia put down a revolt of the large landowners, or hacendados. They fled to the interior of the country and never again threatened Francia or his government.

(Map Source: US State Department)

Paraguay suffered a catastrophic defeat in a war with its larger neighbors—Brazil, Uruguay, and Argentina—that lasted for six years and destroyed much of the development that had been achieved.

Paraguay was now a land of small, medium, and large farms producing a variety of food crops. Some of the farms were owned by the government. A government agency bought all imports and exports. Paraguay exported small quantities of wood, tobacco, sugar, and mate. (Mate is the name of a leaf used to prepare a mildly stimulating drink similar to tea or coffee.)

Francia's Paraguay appears to have made the welfare of its people the first priority. The Guarani Indian peasant consumed a variety and abundance of food. Every Paraguayan was taught to read. Paraguay became the first Latin American nation to eliminate illiteracy. Crime and violence were unknown.

Francia believed that lightly populated Paraguay could only survive in isolation. He did not allow foreigners or foreign influence to enter the country. Francia discovered and destroyed all groups who conspired against him or his policies. Paraguay was the only Latin American country where jails were filled with rich, rather than poor, people.

After nearly forty years in power, Francia died in 1840. He left no will, no heirs, and no money. He was perhaps the only example of a Latin American dictator who did not grow rich while holding power.

Francia's successor, Carlos Antonio Lopez, came from the hacendado class that Francia had defeated and sent fleeing to their estates in 1820. Lopez increased international trade and invited foreign technicians to help Paraguay build railroads, telegraph lines, shipyards, and a small armaments industry. Paraguayan capital paid for the country's new industries. Paraguay did not ask for, did not accept, and did not need foreign loans.

Francisco Solano Lopez succeeded his father, who died in 1862. The new president made the mistake of leading his country into war against Brazil, Uruguay, and Argentina. Lopez seemed to have believed that since Paraguay was a united nation with a healthy, literate population it could defeat these less prosperous and badly organized countries. At this time, Brazil was primarily a big plantation worked by slaves. Brazilian patriotism was so weak that slaves had to be recruited into the army sent to fight in Paraguay. Argentina was a disunited country. Dozens of armed uprisings took place *inside* Argentina while it fought against its neighbor Paraguay. Uruguay was divided by a civil war.

Francisco Solano Lopez seriously overestimated Paraguay's military power. Argentina, Brazil, and Uruguay, helped by British loans, destroyed his country in a brutal war that lasted six years (1864-1870). The Paraguayan people overwhelmingly supported their government. Three out of every four Paraguayans and President Lopez himself died during the war. A population of eight hundred thousand was reduced to two hundred thousand, nearly all of whom were women and children. Only four thousand males older than ten years survived this holocaust. The victorious nations of Brazil and Argentina made the defeated Paraguay give them about half its national territory.

Paraguay may have been the most successful of all Latin American nations between 1813 and 1864, the years between the winning of independence and the beginning of the war against Argentina, Brazil, and Uruguay. During this period, no other Latin American nation matched Paraguay's political and economic independence and internal peace.

Paraguay was a small nation. Its only strength was its ability to be an example for other Latin American nations to study. The policy of Francia and the first Lopez wisely kept Paraguay out of its neighbors' quarrels. The younger Francisco Solano Lopez abandoned this policy. The war he started ruined his country and its unique development.

✗ EXAMPLES TO BE REMEMBERED

The Palmares runaway slave communities and Francia's Paraguay have been rediscovered and written about in today's Latin America. They need to be set beside such famous independence period events as Father Hidalgo's Mexican Revolution, the successful Haitian slave revolt that created a new nation, and the military campaigns of Simón Bolívar across northern South America that helped give independence to at least five South American nations. All these examples stand out as homemade achievements that inspire Latin Americans as they try to build better societies in the 1980s.

4

MODERN TIMES

AN INTRODUCTION TO MODERN LATIN AMERICA

For fifty years after independence (1825-1875), a small group of large landowners, merchants, churchmen, and soldiers dominated the economic system, the politics, and the society of Latin America. After 1875, a new group of small-scale industrialists began to appear in some Latin American countries. They saw a chance to make money by adding home-produced manufactured goods to the crops and cattle of haciendas, fazendas, and plantations. The output of mines also greatly increased after 1875. Foreign investors and foreign companies were quick to penetrate the growing and profitable Latin American mining economy.

Factories and mines created a new working class. One goal of workers has been to organize labor unions to defend themselves. Latin American unions have largely been organized by miners, by city industrial workers, and, in some areas, by plantation workers. Little or no union organization took place among peons living on traditional haciendas or peasant families scratching out a meager livelihood on a few acres. Hacendados and fazendeiros have nearly always reacted to rural labor unions with violent, armed resistance. Therefore, when peasants finally create organizations to defend their interests, these organizations sometimes pursue violent, revolutionary goals.

The military officer and the Latin American armed forces

have continued to be powerful. The original Latin American armies were often ragged but brave units fighting for independence. They were led by daring, astute individuals who were not afraid to seize power and who usually ruled in behalf of the large landowning class. Today's armed forces still intervene in politics and seize power. Usually, the general who emerges as president is the most senior commander. He has been slowly promofed through the ranks to the top of the military hierarchy and is often near retirement. He usually has great respect for the skills of technocrats such as engineers and economists. He is mainly concerned with internal security, revolutionary guerrilla movements, and economic growth. He may still devote most of his energies to defending the interests of one class, such as the large landowner class, but he is more likely to be interested in making all the key sectors of a complex economy—electric power, transportation, industry, mining, banking, and agriculture—safe and secure.

These military dictator presidents are the leaders of central governments or central states. These governments lost power during the nineteenth century, but they have recovered it in this century. Latin American governments have never been more powerful or ambitious than during the second half of the twentieth century. They are more active in striving to maintain order and in directing the economy than they have ever been. Governments hunt down guerrilla warriors who seek to bring about revolution. They construct, own, and manage steel and oil industries. They build roads, hydroelectric power plants, hospitals, and schools. They set up pension and health plans. They establish colonies in empty lands on frontier areas. They sometimes break up or abolish labor unions.

Today's Latin American governments usually want rapid economic growth. That is why they often invite foreign businessmen to establish industries that manufacture a wide variety of products such as automobiles, rubber tires,

(United Nations photo)

Rapid population growth and uneven economic development have characterized Latin America in modern times.

pharmaceuticals, radios, telephones, and paints. But governments tend to view with suspicion foreign businessmen who want to develop oil fields or mines. Latin American governments want these and other precious, non-renewable natural resources to be under their own control. Economic development is probably the biggest concern of present Latin American governments. Economic development in Latin America is more and more defined as creating enough jobs for the economically active or job-seeking population. Since most Latin American countries have a high rate of unemployment—between fifteen and thirty percent—this definition of economic development makes sense for a government that hopes to keep power.

POPULATION GROWTH AND MODERN HISTORY

Rapid population growth may be the key to understanding the bad results of economic development and the problems of modern Latin America. Today's rapidly growing Latin American population reverses the trend of the region's earlier history. During the colonial period, people were often in short supply. In the century following the Spanish conquest, the Indian population may have declined twenty-fold. That is, for every twenty Indians in 1500, only one remained in 1600. Colonial Spanish officials and clergymen feared that the Indian might disappear entirely. In order to stop the decline, the Spanish government sometimes isolated Indian communities by not allowing Europeans or non-Indians to enter them. Perhaps this isolation prevented future epidemics of European diseases such as smallpox.

In Brazil, groups of mestizos, called *bandeirantes*, who lived in São Paulo near the Atlantic coast regularly hunted Indians deep in the interior of the South American wilderness. Captured Indians were marched to the coast and made slaves. Indian slave hunting expeditions could be highly profitable when a population was small.

The rapid growth of the Latin American population dates from the end of the eighteenth century. Between 1800 and 1900, the population tripled, growing from approximately twenty to sixty million. Only the United States and Canada grew faster, increasing their numbers from approximately six to sixty-three million people.

During the twentieth century, Latin America has moved ahead of every other region of the world in the rate of population growth. The number of its people grew from sixty to 360 million between 1900 and 1980. There are now too many people in Latin America. It is no longer possible to earn money hunting and capturing human beings. Instead, poor Latin Americans pay bus companies or truck drivers to take them to large cities where they hope to find jobs. In Brazil, large landowners or private companies with claims to land hire gunmen or pay local police officials to expel landless squatter settlers and their families. The squatters are persons who only want to plant, raise, and harvest crops. They do not want to join millions of unemployed or under-employed people in large cities.

Population may be the key to understanding modern Latin America's problems because the growing population makes possible the payment of low wages in the farming, mining, and manufacturing economies of Latin America. When there are more economically active people than there are jobs, wages may be reduced or kept low. Low wages, in turn, create widespread poverty. Poverty is the principal modern problem of Latin America.

During the twentieth century, Latin Americans have grown acutely aware that human poverty is their most serious problem. They have tried to end poverty by pursuing rapid economic growth. The programs for economic growth seem to have serious flaws since poverty remains an over-whelming fact of life for the majority of the population, even while economies grow rapidly. One Latin American military dictator president summarized the problem of his country, where so many people continued to remain poor despite a booming economy. He said, "The economy goes well, but the people go badly." More and more, Latin Americans question and doubt whether they have followed the correct programs of economic growth.

THREE PHASES OF ECONOMIC GROWTH, 1825-1984

Since independence, Latin America has gone through at least three phases of economic growth and development. The strength and weaknesses of this economic growth becomes evident when one studies its history.

The first phase had already begun during the independence era and lasted well into the twentieth century in some countries. During this phase, Latin American countries produced raw materials (oil, copper, tin, and nitrates) and foods (sugar, coffee, bananas, and chocolate) for export and processing in foreign lands. These foreign countries were the rapidly developing nations of Western Europe, the United States, and Canada. In exchange, Latin American countries received finished manufactured products.

During the second phase, Latin American countries continued to export raw materials and unprocessed food, but they also began to produce many of the manufactured goods they had previously imported. Clothing of all types, canned foods, furniture, and simple tools began to be made at home rather than imported. As long as the manufactured products required no advanced engineering skills or large investments, they could be produced in Latin America. At the same time, complicated, expensive machines such as power looms, used to weave cloth, were imported. Automobiles, refrigerators, power generators and machine tools were also acquired.

The second phase began in countries such as Brazil,

Argentina, Chile, and Mexico as early as 1875, and it still continues today. We may think of this phase in two ways: It involved the initial steps taken in the process of industrialization, and it was an effort to make some manufactured products at home instead of importing them.

Phase three began quite recently. We can find its origins in the 1920s and 1930s, but it is primarily a process that dates from the end of World War II. In this phase, Latin America, in effect, told the world that it was dissatisfied with phase one and even phase two. It was no longer willing to export raw materials and unprocessed foods for finished manufactured goods; nor would Latin America be satisfied with making a few of its needed manufactured goods. In this third phase, the Latin American countries served notice that they, too, intended to have economies that were highly productive and well-balanced. They, too, would have the majority of their populations clustered in urban centers and employed in thousands of busy factories, shops, and office buildings. Not only clothing and canned foods, but automobiles, cement, refrigerators, and finished metals were to be made at home rather than imported. The countryside would thrive as never before with peons and peasants becoming a class of prosperous farmers who fed growing city populations.

The third phase is well advanced in many Latin American countries. Nobody can be sure whether this third phase will finally overcome poverty or whether it will produce the disappointing results of the first two phases. In order to understand the problems of recent and present-day Latin America, we need to examine more closely certain details of each of these three phases.

Phase One

At one time, Latin Americans were taught that they were fortunate to have a large supply of land, year-round warm weather, and a plentiful supply of workers. They considered

themselves blessed to have vast deposits of tin, copper, iron ore, and petroleum. Lacking knowledge of advanced processes of manufacturing and without skilled workers, Latin Americans believed that they could still prosper by selling minerals and unprocessed foods to the people of the industrial countries. With the monies earned from the sale of such products, they could import the manufactured goods they needed. Such simple strategies usually turned out to be mistaken. The story of Guatemala's bananas and Bolivia's tin illustrate the built-in weaknesses of phase one.

In 1899, a group of fruit companies in the United States joined together to form the United Fruit Company. The countries of Central America allowed them to enter, take over vast acres of unpopulated lowland areas, and develop banana plantations.

Guatemala was one of these countries. The United Fruit Company obtained rights to thousands of acres of empty, unhealthful, tropical lowlands, first along the Caribbean and, later, the Pacific coasts of Guatemala. The company leveled the forests and planted the cleared land with bananas. It eradicated the malaria-carrying mosquito. It built railroads from the banana plantations to newly established ports on the Caribbean coast. It even built a railroad connecting the area with the distant capital of Guatemala City. It persuaded Mayan Indians and other peasants to leave their homes in the highlands and become the workers in this now healthful lowland zone. These workers were paid wages three or four times higher than the national average. Their housing was superior to what they had known. For the first time, modern medical care was available to them. Meanwhile, the Guatemalan government collected tax revenues from the sale of bananas. It was thereby able to pay the salaries of the army and government employees as well as the interest and principal on the foreign debt. In short, Guatemala had apparently taken a significant step forward.

But further developments did not bear out Guatemala's high hopes. Eventually, the banana trees either exhausted the soil or were struck by a deadly blight. The plantations had to be abandoned, and planting shifted to the other side of the country. Many of the workers remained behind. They were no longer well-paid plantation workers. They now used the forsaken fields to cultivate enough food for their own survival. They were once again poor people. After seventy years of flourishing banana plantations, a distinguished geographer summarized the results: "Guatemala is still a country of very poor farmers. . . . Of the total population of Guatemala, seventy-five percent are rural and more than seventy percent are illiterate. The great majority of the rural people are subsistence farmers who produce nothing for sale, and who are able to supply themselves with only about a third of what the experts think is a minimum diet for the maintenance of health."[1]

In Bolivia, another industry, the tin industry, prospered greatly. Let us see what this prosperity did for Bolivia.

First we should note that Bolivian tin mines were not developed by a foreign company. The story of Bolivian tin begins with the efforts of a Bolivian, Simon Patiño. Born in 1864, he was a mestizo. Although three of his grandparents were Aymará Indians, Patiño preferred Western ways of life to the Aymará Indian ways.

As a young man, Patiño was a hard-working owner of a mule train that transported goods over the mountainous terrain of southwestern Bolivia. There is a story that one of his customers could not pay a transportation charge and gave Patiño part of an abandoned mine in payment. The new mine owner promptly went to work, and soon his property was producing a considerable quantity of tin. With the profits, he purchased other mining properties. By the first decade of the twentieth century, he owned the largest tin deposits in the

1.   Preston James, *Latin America* (New York, 1969), p. 141.

world. As the tin can became a worldwide commodity, Patiño's mines produced more and more tin, and he accumulated more and more wealth. By the middle of the 1920s, he was one of the six wealthiest men in the world.

Patiño left Bolivia in 1922. Between 1922 and 1940, he served first as Bolivian ambassador to Spain and then as ambassador to France. In 1940, he moved to New York, where he died in 1947. He seldom returned to Bolivia, although he built three palatial residences for himself in his native country.

Bolivia is still well-known for its tin, and minerals are still its most important exports. But tin did little to develop Bolivia economically, judging from the economic state of the country in 1952, when a revolutionary government seized the tin mines. The taxes on thirty to forty thousand tons of tin exported every year from 1925 to 1950 may have helped the national treasury pay its bills, but neither Patiño nor any of the other wealthy mine owners used their profits to establish new industries in Bolivia. All the ore was exported to Europe or the United States for processing. The miners were Aymará Indians recruited from their native villages. They were paid low wages—certainly lower than the banana plantation workers in Guatemala. They suffered from malnutrition, and one-third of them contracted silicosis, a miners' disease that attacks and destroys the lungs.

After half a century of tin mining, the following summary was written of Bolivian economic development: "Before 1952, the minority of wealthy landowners and mine owners, along with the higher officers of the army, lived in a world apart. The great majority of the inhabitants of Bolivia were Indian farmers who remained essentially outside the system of buying and selling." Bolivia remains one of the three poorest countries in Latin America—that is, it is one of the economically least developed of all Latin American countries.

Bolivia and Guatemala are two Latin American countries that adopted the first phase strategy of seeking prosperity by exporting a raw material or an unprocessed food. With the monies earned from these exports, a few necessary, finished manufactured products and luxury items could be imported. This approach generated great profits for a few, but little or no economic and social development for the majority. Latin Americans have long complained that they do not have underdeveloped countries, only underdeveloped people. How many Guatemalans and Bolivians became literate, healthy, skilled people as a result of their nation's plantation or mining prosperity? Surely not enough to allow either country even to approach the status of a developed nation. What happened when the plantation whithered away because of a crop disease or exhausted soil? In Guatemala, formerly well-paid plantation workers once again became subsistence farmers. What happens when a tin mine or oil well is exhausted? The nation is left with a hole in the ground and often little else.

In the first phase, the prosperity of the mining or plantation economy was shared by a tiny minority of the population. It was often confined to a single region or district of the country. Meanwhile, the mass of the country's people continued to live in the poverty they had known for centuries. Their lives were practically untouched by these isolated islands of temporarily productive and highly profitable mines or plantations.

Phase Two

Productive and profitable mines and plantations are not evils in themselves. The income they produce, the jobs they provide, and the taxes they pay can make important contributions to the economic growth and development of any country. But every country needs a people and economic system that produce more than raw materials and unprocessed foods for export. Latin Americans themselves have realized this for a long time. That is why they have struggled to escape dependence on one or two exported crops or raw materials and to take the first steps toward industrialization.

Initial industrialization began in countries such as Brazil, Argentina, Chile, and Mexico as early as the 1870s. This first phase lasted until the 1930s, when the industrial world, led by the United States, plunged into the most serious of all the modern depressions.

During the period from 1870-1930, easy-to-make and widely used products that would otherwise be imported began to be manufactured within Latin America. Shirts and shoes, canned and bottled foods and drinks, furniture, kitchen utensils, and bathtubs were among these products. The factories or workshops that produced them cost relatively little to build and equip. Production did not require highly skilled labor or much technical know-how. Manufactured products that required no advanced engineering skills or large investments were selected to be made in Latin America. However, the manufacturing process was not an independent Latin American development. The machines and equipment used in the factories or workshops had to be imported. For example, Latin Americans manufactured clothing on power looms imported from Great Britain or the United States.

The most serious obstacle to industrialization was not the absence of capital, skilled workers, natural resources, technology, or engineering skills. It was the size of the home market. This market consisted of the minority of people who earned money and bought goods. For the most part, this market existed and grew only in large towns and cities. Until 1945, the majority of Latin Americans lived at the subsistence level; they did not have the income to spend on manufactured products. The capacity of Latin American industry to expand has been limited, and continues to be limited, by the fact that so many millions of people do not earn enough to buy the output of factories.

The history of industrialization in São Paulo, Brazil, from

1870 to 1930 can help us to understand the relationship between a small market, people living at the subsistence level, and limited industrial expansion.

São Paulo is a state that lies in the south-central part of Brazil. It contains nearly twenty-three million people, which makes it more populous than all other Latin American countries except Mexico, Argentina, and Colombia. The state and city of São Paulo constitute one of the largest industrial parks of Latin America. In them are concentrated at least forty thousand industrial establishments that employ 850 thousand workers. It took little more than a century for São Paulo to reach this level.

Perhaps the most remarkable years of growth occurred between 1900 and 1930. During that period, the number of industrial establishments soared from two hundred to eleven thousand. Cotton clothing, leather goods, hats, refined sugar, cereals, beer, soft drinks, furniture, tiles, cement, nails, plate glass, plumbing fixtures, pots, pans, and paper were some of the locally manufactured goods produced during this boom. Yet, there was a built-in limitation to all this expansion. The businessmen and industrialists of São Paulo were ready and eager to produce manufactured goods that did not require the most advanced skills and machinery, but they were not ready, for example, to produce their own machinery. Generally, they imported the machinery used in their factories.

The story of a local citizen, Evaristo Engelberg, who invented a coffee huller in the 1880s illustrates this deficiency. The coffee huller removes the outer covering of a coffee bean and then grinds it. Since São Paulo was the world's leading producer of coffee, such a machine could have been used locally. However, no Brazilian was able or willing to establish a factory that would make this relatively complicated machine. Therefore, Engelberg sold his machine to a group of North Americans who established a plant in Buffalo, New York, to produce the coffee huller. It was then marketed throughout the world, including Brazil.

The story of the coffee huller demonstrates that São Paulo's businessmen were not willing to take the process of industrialization beyond producing certain inexpensive, simple products for the home market with machines imported from industrial countries. São Paulo businessmen did not believe Brazil could be an independent industrial center producing its own equipment, tools, and machines. They could not export ground coffee to the United States since a high tariff protected the US food processing industry. The output of São Paulo's manufacturing industries would be limited to the Brazilian market.

The São Paulo industrialists also shared the familiar problem of a home market that did not grow. The São Paulo factories built before 1920 underwent little or no modernization during the next thirty years. Most owners did not replace their equipment or expand their production. During the worldwide depression of the 1930s, the majority of them worked to prevent the importation of new plant or factory equipment. These industrialists believed that they could not survive if some producers bought new machines and turned out goods more cheaply. These conservative industrialists also wanted to limit the length of the work day. The idea was to limit factory output during a depression in order to help weak and strong firms survive in a market that did not grow.

During the period from 1920-1950, the São Paulo businessman lived with the knowledge that the Brazilian market had a limited capacity to absorb industrially manufactured products. He knew that roughly forty percent of the Brazilian population lived outside the commercial economy, that there were extensive regions of rural Brazil where peasants went for years without seeing or handling money and where there was illiteracy and almost total ignorance of Brazil's new industrial economy and what it produced.

Phase Three—Industrialization Since 1930

By 1930, a half century of Latin American industrialization seemed to have reached a point where there could be no further growth. Nevertheless, Latin Americans did not abandon the idea of industrialization. Other attempts to produce economic growth and developed countries seemed to lead nowhere. That plantation and mining economies were unacceptable alternatives had been demonstrated by the history of bananas in Central America and tin in Bolivia.

Factory owners, factory workers, and their supporters insisted that industrialization remained the best way to create wealth and jobs. They argued that no other form of development could transform a society. Successful industrialization forced a vast movement of people from rural to urban areas. It brought about the expansion and rebuilding of cities. It made societies wealthier and more powerful.

These ideas about the benefits of industrialization influenced several groups in Latin America. The hopes and ambitions of these Latin Americans have in turn influenced governments. Since 1930, governments have promoted industrialization with growing enthusiasm.

Governments have tried many approaches. In 1940, the President of Brazil, Getulio Vargas, decided that the Brazilian paper industry was not producing enough newsprint. He knew that the growing number of Brazilian newspapers had to import newsprint. Therefore, he persuaded the largest newspaper and magazine publisher in Brazil to ask the Klabin family, owners of a paper mill in São Paulo, to expand their production.

At first, the Klabin family hesitated. Their paper mill was successful enough as it was. What guarantee would there be that a great increase in its output would be consumed in Brazil? They also needed a railroad line to connect their mill with distant pine forests that provided the raw materials for paper. President Vargas promised the Klabins a loan for new

(United Nations photo/Sweinn Einarsson)

Latin American governments have pressed hard for industrial development in order to become independent of foreign resources and to create new wealth.

machinery, a guaranteed market, and the railroad spur. The family then agreed to expand their paper mill.

About the same time (1939), Chile was setting up a government corporation to encourage many businesses, both large and small. It was called the *Corporacion de Fomento* (FOMENTO). With monies obtained from taxes and from the United States Export-Import Bank, Chile's FOMENTO granted loans to industry, mining, agriculture, and fisheries to help them expand their output. To one group of fishermen, FOMENTO supplied nets and boats to replace the hooks and lines they had previously used. The fishermen so increased their production that fresh fish became available for the first time in the large interior capital of Santiago. Money was also provided to help landowners purchase United States-made farm machinery and better breeds of cattle and sheep. In this way, FOMENTO helped the land and the ocean yield more food for a hungry and growing Chilean population.

Argentina established an ambitious development corporation in 1946. It was called the Argentine Institute for the Promotion of Exchange (IAPI). It had the task of buying wheat and beef from Argentine farmers at a lower price than they received in the world market. IAPI then sold the wheat and beef on the world market and realized a large profit. This profit was invested in expanding Argentine industry. For example, money was earmarked for new hydroelectric power plants, since the expansion of Argentine industry was being hampered by the shortage of electric power.

IAPI seemed to be a sound idea, but it made one crucial mistake: It tried to make too much money too quickly. As a result, it paid farmers and ranchers too little for their wheat and beef. The farmers and ranchers retaliated. They planted less wheat and allowed their herds to shrink. The Argentine government suddenly found that it did not have enough of these basic foods both to sell abroad and to feed its people at home. The government introduced meatless days in 1952.

Such forced dieting was unheard of in previously well-fed Argentina and stirred strong opposition to the government. The failure of the IAPI scheme may have been an important factor leading to the overthrow, in 1955, of the government that had sponsored it.

The Extent of Government Involvement

Chile's FOMENTO and Argentina's IAPI are just two examples of the ways governments have intervened to encourage economic growth and development. Such intervention may take the form of supplying a loan to people who want to start a new factory. In other instances, governments have formed national corporations, which they then help to manage and fund in an effort to start an important industry. Usually this kind of public corporation establishes or runs basic industries, such as those that produce steel, oil, or hydroelectric power.

Steel

During the 1940s, the Brazilian government helped to build and then to run the giant Volta Redonda steel mills. The Chilean government oversaw the building of the Huachipato steel center, completed in 1950. Huachipato included a new, modern industrial city with up-to-date, comfortable housing for steel workers and plant managers. Fifteen other factories that used steel in final products were also established in this special industrial city. The whole achievement could not have happened without the participation of the Chilean government, which arranged for the funding. Similarly, the Colombian government sponsored the building of a national steel plant at Paz del Rio. The decision to build the Paz del Rio plant was criticized by foreign experts. They said that the steel mill would be unprofitable. In spite of such warnings, the government went ahead, borrowing the needed capital from European sources. Paz del Rio was completed in 1956. By the middle of the 1970s, this national steel plant was both productive and profitable, and it supplied Colombia with half of its raw steel.

Oil

Latin American governments have also been trying to set up oil industries in their countries. In the past, governments invited foreign oil companies to enter their countries in order to find oil fields and to drill wells. The foreign companies had the right to pump, refine, and sell the oil, usually paying a relatively small tax to the government.

Latin Americans now believe that oil is too important a resource to be left in the hands of foreigners. They fear that foreign oil companies will exhaust the supply to meet the demand for oil in foreign industrialized countries. If that should happen, there may not be enough oil to run the growing industries of Latin America. With these fears in mind, Latin American governments have moved to bring the oil industries under their control. Mexico moved first. It seized the foreign-owned oil industry in 1938. Since that time a government corporation, called PEMEX, has run the industry. In 1968, the Peruvian government seized the oil installations of the United States-owned International Petroleum Corporation. During the 1970s, the government of oil rich Venezuela legislated the return of foreign oil concessions to its control.

The most complicated case of oil nationalism may be that of Brazil. In 1953 the Brazilian government created a national petroleum refining corporation, PETROBRAS. This corporation maintained a monopoly over Brazil's oil industry until 1975, when the nation's military dictatorship opened the country to prospecting by foreign oil companies under risk contracts. That is, the foreign companies would risk their money drilling for oil. If they discovered it, they had the right to reap profits.

The decision was politically risky. The government feared a popular reaction and a reaction within the army. A generation of Brazilians had been taught that their oil must be a nationally-owned monopoly. No great reaction occurred. However, the foreign companies drilling in Atlantic coastal waters have not yet discovered bonanza-sized oil fields.

Modern Latin American governments find themselves strongly criticized and even threatened by local groups when they permit foreigners to control oil or other key natural resources. One reason for the overthrow of the Argentine government in 1955 was that it had signed an agreement allowing a foreign company to enter and develop Argentine oil fields. In 1983, Chile's anti-Communist, military dictatorship provoked popular protests when it threatened to return Chile's copper mines to previous foreign owners.

Hydroelectric Power

Electricity is an important source of power for the machines of industry. For some time, Latin American governments have struggled to increase the output of electricity. Sometimes, as in Colombia, they have built dams in a major river valley. Colombia's Cauca Valley Corporation, modeled after the Tennessee Valley Authority of the United States, has been a great success and supplies power for the rapidly growing industrial city of Cali.

Attempts to increase electricity have not usually been accompanied by dramatic government seizures of foreign firms, as has been the case with oil. Nevertheless, Latin American governments appear to be uncomfortable with this major source of power is in the hands of foreigners. Brazil took over some foreign-owned power companies in 1962, although it agreed to pay the former owners. In 1963, it created a public corporation, ELECTROBRAS, to promote expansion of electric power. Fidel Castro's Cuba went further. It seized the foreign-controlled electric power industry in 1960 without compensating the owners.

The largest Latin American hydroelectric project is the colossal Itaipu power dam built on the Paraná river that serves as a frontier between Brazil and Paraguay. Itaipu is a joint Brazilian-Paraguayan government project. Finished in 1983, the dam is as tall as a sixty-story building and has created an artificial lake more than a hundred miles long. It will produce twenty-five percent more electricity than the largest United States power dam when all of its turbines and generators are finally installed in 1989.

Itaipu is particularly important for Paraguay. When a Paraguayan engineer explained that before Itaipu, Paraguay was condemned to underdevelopment, he meant that without oil, coal, or rivers inside the country, Paraguay could never produce cheap power to run an industrial park. With the electric power of Itaipu, Paraguay has the chance to be a developed or industrial nation. This statement recalls how strongly many Latin Americans interpret the process of industrialization as being equal to development.

FOREIGN INVESTORS
AND ECONOMIC GROWTH

Most Latin American governments seem to believe that their countries cannot reach a high rate of economic growth without outside help. They seek money and aid from the governments of rich countries such as the United States, West Germany, and Japan—and especially from foreign international banks and multinational corporations.

Foreign investors have long been present in Latin America. After independence, for example, they immediately began to purchase Latin American government bonds. These bonds were usually offered for sale in London in order to pay a government's everyday expenses or debts. Because most

Latin American governments were unstable, the bonds sold
as high risk investments. Governments almost always had to
accept much less than the bonds' face value; sometimes they
received less than sixty percent. Nevertheless, they were
obliged to repay the full value of the bonds, plus interest on
this value. If a government was unable to pay, powerful
creditor nations might intervene. In 1905, for example, the
United States forced the Dominican Republic to allow
American authorities to collect its import taxes. The United
States gave forty-five percent to the Dominican government,
while turning over fifty-five percent to foreign creditors.

During the period from 1825-1875, most foreign investment in Latin America was in government bonds. From
1875 to 1930, foreign investment or foreign capital primarily
served to help construct railroads, trolley lines, and better
port facilities or to install public utilities such as electric
power and telephone systems. Foreign investors also acquired
important mining properties, such as nitrate (a source of
fertilizers and explosives) and copper mines in Chile.
Eventually, they also controlled oil drilling rights in Venezuela and Mexico. The effect of all this foreign investment
was to integrate the Latin American economy more tightly
into the world market and to establish new profitable systems
of transportation and communication in Latin America—all
under foreign control.

The phase of foreign investment that began in the 1870s
was sharply checked by the Great Depression of the 1930s.
World trade and industrial output shrunk. Foreign investors
saw few new opportunities to make money in Latin America.

World War II (1939-1945) ended the depression. During
the war, American and European investors were deeply
involved in the survival struggles of their own countries.
They could not make new investments in Latin America.
Nevertheless, the Latin American economies benefitted
because the warring industrial nations needed Latin American
resources. Latin Americans sold large quantities of raw

materials and foodstuffs at high prices. At the end of the war, some Latin American countries had large amounts of foreign currency owed to them. By 1950, five years after the end of the war, most of this money had been spent. It went either to pay for foreign-owned railroad, electric power and telephone systems; to buy imported luxury goods for rich consumers; or to pay for newly imported factory equipment.

After 1950, a new drive for industrialization greatly increased opportunities for foreign investors. Latin American governments made special efforts to persuade foreign companies to start or expand industries. The process of industrialization soon became a triple partnership between local capitalists, Latin American governments, and foreign companies.

Multinational Corporations

Foreign investment has grown dramatically in every decade since 1950. It comes largely from multinational companies. A multinational company owns and operates firms in more than one country. The Latin American multinational companies are branches of firms whose headquarters or principal production, research, and development centers are almost always in the United States, Canada, Japan or Western Europe. The United States Ford Motor Company and the Volkswagen Company of West Germany are two examples of multinational motor vehicle firms with plants in Latin America.

Since 1950, dozens of multinational firms with home offices in the United States, Canada, Japan, Great Britain, West Germany, France, the Netherlands, and Italy have established control over key areas of many Latin American national economies. These areas include transportation (automobiles, trucks, and buses), pharmaceuticals, chemicals, food processing, electrical equipment, and computers.

Multinational companies exercise control over their branches from outside Latin America. An extreme case of outside control can be seen in the American-owned IBM computer factory in Campinas, Brazil. The factory is connected to a computer in the United States. The United States-based computer thinks for the Brazilian IBM factory.

Why the Multinationals Are in Latin America

Several factors explain the presence of multinational branch firms in Latin America. High profitability is the first. Multinational firms usually earn higher rates of profits on Latin American investments than on investments in home countries.

Government tariff and import policies may be another factor. A Latin American government may want to manufacture a certain commodity at home. It will then either prohibit the commodity's import or levy so high a tax on its import that the good will be priced out of the local market. The multinational firm must produce in the Latin American country or lose this market.

Latin American governments will encourage an invasion of multinational companies when they want to speed up industrialization. They will offer the incentives of low taxes. A military dictatorship might act to keep wages low and to outlaw strikes.

Latin American governments realize that a multinational firm can create an industry virtually overnight. One year a Latin American nation imports automobiles; the next year its workers produce Fords, Fiats, and Volkswagens for the local market; and the next year the country is exporting automobiles and trucks.

This process may benefit local producers because the multinational branch may gradually create a chain of local production that includes national firms as links. Originally, Mexico only required that foreign automobile firms assemble cars in Mexico. The Ford Motor Company or the General Motor Corporation could import some or all of the parts used in the assembly of a car. Later, the Mexican government insisted that more and more of the parts be made in Mexico. This strategy allowed Mexican national firms to emerge and grow as suppliers of brakes, springs, seats, radiators, carburetors, and other automobile and truck parts.

Multinational branch firms are also welcomed because they create jobs. The jobs in their factories expand the income and size of the Latin American working class. Better paying management jobs offer opportunities for the middle class. For these reasons, the working and middle classes seldom oppose the entry of multinational companies.

Finally, multinational firms usually produce quality goods, which means that they meet an international standard of excellence. These high quality commodities appeal to middle- and upper-class Latin American consumers who can afford them and who compare themselves to consumers in developed industrial countries.

Multinational companies clearly have their own reasons for wanting to establish branches in Latin America. However, they are also wooed by Latin American countries that are trying to speed up or start the process of industrialization. They are welcomed by local capitalists who hope to establish supply companies. They are welcomed by workers who seek jobs. Finally, their presence comforts consumers who want to buy high quality goods. With so many groups in favor of multinationals, they have become securely established throughout Latin America. Nevertheless, Latin Americans often criticize them.

Criticism of Multinational Companies

Latin American critics argue that multinationals invest little foreign capital in Latin America. Instead of bringing American dollars or German *marks*, the multinationals use

local money—Mexican *pesos or* Brazilian *cruzeiros*—to
finance their investments. Multinational banks operating in
Latin America are charged with capturing local capital and
lending it to multinational manufacturing companies. Little
capital remains for local national firms.

Another criticism is that while multinational firms create
jobs, they pay their workers only one-fifth or one-third of the
salaries they pay in industrial countries such as the United
States and West Germany. Salaries are said to be low
because multinationals cooperate with Latin American
military dictatorships that repress or outlaw labor unions or
that do not permit strikes or collective bargaining between
workers and management. Multinationals answer that they
pay relatively low salaries because local wages are low.

Multinational firms are also accused of profiteering and of
illegally sending profits out of Latin America. They are said
to overcharge for the transfer of technology in order to get
around Latin American laws that limit the percentage of
profits that can be sent or remitted out of the country.
Technology refers to the patents, processes, chemical formulas, engineering designs, and equipment used in manufacturing. It is said to be transferred when its owner sells or
licenses its use to another company. Such transfer arrange-
ments can even take place within multinational companies.
Hence, a Latin American branch might pay for the technology
developed by its distant parent company.

Multinationals sometimes sell equipment and parts manufactured in Latin America to home country plants at below
cost. A United States automobile firm might charge seventy
percent of the price of a motor made in a Latin American
subsidiary for use on a Detroit assembly line. This book-
keeping trick is one more way of getting around laws that do
not permit multinational companies to send home profits
above a certain rate. Latin Americans argue that multinationals must obey these laws in order to build up the supply
of capital in Latin America.

Yet another criticism is that the multinationals develop all their new products and technology outside of Latin America. The Latin American branch or subsidiary will not have its own research and development program. A Latin American computer engineer who works for a West German multinational electrical equipment firm complains that he and other engineers are not allowed to do more than routine work. All the thinking and technology comes from West Germany. The company does not need or want Latin American research and thinking. The engineer questions whether Latin America will ever acquire technological independence to go with its political independence.

A final criticism of multinationals is that they enter a Latin American market and destroy a competing national firm by offering a better, and perhaps cheaper, version of a product. They may also purchase a national company because the Latin American managers or owners believe that they cannot compete and must sell.

THE FUTURE OF NATIONAL CAPITALISM

Latin Americans have long debated whether a foreign company with more capital, better technology, and an outstanding final product is preferable to a nationally-owned firm that produces a usable, though perhaps inferior, product. In the 1880s, Chile's President José Manuel Balmaceda defended national over imported manufactured goods. He argued that Chile must follow the example of the United States and "consume our own national production, although it may not be as perfect and as finished as the foreign." In 1891, Balmaceda was overthrown by an armed uprising financed by the British owner of most of Chile's nitrate mines.

In 1979, Antônio Emirio de Moraes, the owner and director of the largest group of Brazilian national companies, argued that Brazil needed more adding machines and fewer computers. He meant that Brazil's relative economic backwardness made the adding machine an appropriate tool. He believed it was better to manufacture and use products that fit the nation's stage of industrial development than to try to establish instant industrial equality with countries such as the United States, Canada, and Japan.

The nineteenth-century Chilean President José Manuel Balmaceda and the present-day Brazilian businessman Antônio Emirio de Moraes represent the ambitions and the realism of Latin American national capitalists. Latin America has produced tens of thousands of industrial and commercial firms since achieving independence. It has even spawned multinational corporations. The Bolivian Simón Patiño extended his mining business to Great Britain, where he constructed a tin smelter. The Argentine family-owned firm of Bunge & Born is one of the world's largest grain and food processing companies. Bunge & Born has companies operating in dozens of countries, including the United States.

Latin American-born multinationals are not typical of the region. Latin America has always lagged behind the leading industrial countries in technology, capital, business organization, and numbers of literate people. Despite these serious deficits, industrial growth under local capital and local business leaders has been a fact of Latin American history for more than a century. The greater growth and prestige of United States, Canadian, Japanese, French, West German, and British multinational corporations has not eliminated private Latin American capital. It continues in traditional, established industries such as processed foods, textiles, and metallurgy. It grows by linking itself up with multinational firms as suppliers of parts. In some places, private Latin American business groups are even trying to enter highly competitive, new industries that require the most advanced technology and huge investments. In Brazil, several new companies are trying to develop computer firms. One of these companies, Itautec, is a striking example of the continuing potential of private Latin American capital.

Itautec is the acronym for Itau Technology, an electronics company that is part of a conglomerate of more than forty firms. A large commercial bank, the Itau Bank, is included in the conglomerate and is its most profitable unit. Olavo Setubal, an engineer and former mayor of the city of São Paulo, is the long-time president of the conglomerate.

The Itau management first became interested in computers because its bank, with more than one thousand branch offices, was a heavy user of them. This bank had large earnings and almost no debts. Setubal and his managers decided that investing in a company that made computers for the rapidly growing bank would be a good way to spend the bank's profits. In this way, Itautec was established in 1979.

Itautec was entirely created with Brazilian national capital and workers. The company hired Brazilian engineers and technicians to develop its own computer hardware and software. These engineers created a system for designing complex electronic circuits on computers. Itautec chemists formulated a solution for coating the hardware wafer plates on which are mounted the electronic chips that work together to think and remember.

Some equipment had to be imported. The machine that drills electronic circuit patterns in the wafer plates was purchased in the United States. The thinking and remembering electronic chips came from the United States and Japan. In 1983, the Itautec management decided to end its dependency on foreign chips. The management elected to invest as much as $300 million in a computer chip factory.

The original purpose of Itautec was to provide the Itau conglomerate's bank with a computer system. Having achieved this, the company decided to sell the system to other banks. Meanwhile, Itautec had developed a small computer for office and general personal use.

When Itautec moved into the field of selling computers and their programs to other banks and to the general public, it began to compete with long-established multinational firms. The Itau management made this decision knowing that prospective Brazilian clients were biased in favor of multinational-made computers. These computers were seen as high quality products that their makers reliably maintained and serviced. Furthermore, the new Itautec computers were likely to be more expensive than those of their multinational competitors. Developing a new computer required a heavy investment, which Itautec believed it must recover through a high sales price.

What gave the Itau management confidence was a government national security policy that reserved part of the market for computers made by Brazilian national companies. The reserved market was for medium-sized computers, which multinationals would not be able to sell in Brazil. Itautec intended to compete strongly in this market reserved exclusively for Brazilian national models.

Suddenly, the government changed its policy. It announced that Brazil needed to produce a new medium-sized computer sooner than Itautec or other national companies could develop one. The government maintained that if the time were too brief, the Brazilian companies could buy the technology they needed from multinational firms.

The Itautec management reacted strongly. Setubal argued that if his company started to buy technology, it would simply become part of a multinational firm such as IBM. Itautec, other Brazilian firms, and Brazil itself would never achieve autonomy in computer technology and would forever have to depend on foreign computer thinking and systems. What would happen if the outside multinational supplier suddenly decided to stop the flow of critical computer technology?

RESULTS OF ECONOMIC GROWTH
SINCE INDEPENDENCE

The efforts of a group of Brazilian businessmen to found a national computer industry is just one small part of the complicated history of Latin America's economic growth since independence. In the beginning of this period, there were locally owned plantations, haciendas, fazendas, and mines. There were handicraft industries that produced clothing and simple household goods such as dishes and furniture. Since the end of the nineteenth century, factories and banks, along with modern transportation and communication systems, have been added to this old Latin American economy.

Many of the owners of the industries of the new economy have been Latin Americans. Other owners have been foreigners. Since 1950, the desire of different Latin American groups to hasten the pace of industrialization has caused governments and multinational corporations to become leading agents of accelerated economic growth.

Between 1950 and 1980, the rates of economic growth in different Latin American countries have often been high, frequently rising above five percent per year. However, the social results have been less than satisfactory. The vast majority of the Latin American people have not participated in selecting the priorities for a program of economic growth. They have generally had to accept their government's belief that a new factory has higher priority than a new school or health clinic.

Great social sacrifices have been built into the Latin American industrialization programs. Hundreds of large, modern factories turn out billions of dollars' worth of sophisticated goods, but most of the techniques and processes are developed outside and transferred to Latin America. Factories provide millions of jobs, but wages are low. A Latin American factory employee works as hard as an

American or German employee but usually earns about seventy-five percent less. Manufacturing industries do not begin to supply enough jobs for the economically active population. Nor does other work fill the gap left by manufacturing. Additional jobs in agriculture, mining, and service work—which includes everyone from bank tellers and waiters to sanitation workers and teachers—do not provide anything close to full employment. Furthermore, this work often pays less than factory work. After a century of nearly continual economic growth, there are greater numbers of poor Latin Americans than ever.

5

THE CRISIS OF THE 1980s

By the late 1970s, more than twenty years of rapid industrial growth based on an alliance between governments and multinational companies had stalled. The world recession of the early 1980s brought worsening conditions. The Latin American economies went into reverse. One of the worst cases was Peru, where unemployment reached more than fifty percent of the economically active population. Nearly as badly hurt was Chile. The rate of unemployment stood at thirty percent. In Brazil, the number of jobs in 1983 fell to the 1973 level. Tens of thousands of homeless, begging people wandered the streets of Brazil's large cities and searched through garbage for something to eat.

The sharp economic setbacks of the early 1980s struck a generation of Latin Americans who had experienced the highest rates of continual economic growth in the region's history. Between 1960 and 1980, the average annual rate of growth was between five and six percent. The output of the Latin American economies nearly tripled, while income per person nearly doubled. In other words, the Latin American population, though one of the world's fastest growing with an annual rate of increase of nearly three percent, grew at about half the rate of the Latin American economy. Therefore, real income per person increased substantially. But the fruits of rapid economic growth were badly distributed. Economic growth concentrated wealth instead of spreading it more equally.

This concentration of income was extreme. The wealthiest ten percent of the Latin American population received between thirty-five and fifty percent of the region's income in the late 1970s. The poorest forty percent got between seven and fifteen percent. A 1979 World Bank study showed that the richest ten percent of Brazilians received thirty times more income than the poorest forty percent. In Mexico, the proportion was better. The richest ten percent of the people received only fifteen times more than the poorest forty percent. To appreciate this improved income distribution, let us compare it to that of the United States, itself a nation of great extremes in wealth and income: In the United States, the best paid ten percent earned only seven times more than the worst paid forty percent.

Extreme income concentration or inequality translates into absolute poverty for the majority of the Latin American people. Absolute poverty means that people do not have enough income for the food, clothing, and housing they need. In Latin America, nearly two-thirds of all children suffer from malnutrition. If they do not die of starvation, they will grow up with damaged bodies and brains. Some of the worst incidences of malnutrition can be found in Central America. Yet, half of this region's agricultural land produces crops of little or no nutritional value such as sugar and coffee which are grown for export because foreigners have the money to buy them. Low income means that most Central Americans do not have money to buy food crops such as beans, rice, and corn. Neither do they have land on which to raise these crops.

The reason for the presence of so much poverty in Latin America has long been debated. In 1983, the President of Brazil maintained that the cause was high population growth that "devours, as has been observed, economic growth." In fact, statistics show that population growth between 1960 and 1980 devoured only about one-half of the economic growth. A better explanation is the huge gap between income received by the wealthiest ten percent and the poorest forty percent. High economic growth rates do not narrow the gap. In some Latin American countries, high growth rates actually widen it. When accepting the Nobel Peace Prize in 1980, the Argentine architect Adolfo Perez Ezquivel insisted that the rich were getting richer and the poor poorer in Latin America.

Latin American governments generally control income by setting minimum wages. These minimum wages do not usually keep up with increases in prices, which often exceed one hundred percent per year. Minimum wage laws usually state that salaries must be raised annually to equal the rate of price hikes. In reality, governments frequently issue official inflation figures that are lower than true price increases, or they change their laws and try to lower inflation by keeping wage increases low. In 1983, Mexico suffered an official price inflation of one hundred percent, but the government decreed a wage increase of 15.6 percent. The loss in real wages for most Mexican workers threatened to be greater than eighty percent. The government saved itself from a popular revolt with a typical Latin American solution: It subsidized or paid for part of the cost of food and transportation. Despite the inflation, the price of the Mexican *tortilla* did not rise; it continued to sell for fifteen pesos, although it cost thirty-five pesos to make. The government paid the difference. The price of a ride on the Mexico City subway system remained one peso, as it had been ten years earlier. In reality, each ride cost about fourteen pesos. The government made up the difference.

Such subsidies allowed the Mexican government to use inflation to lower salaries without provoking a confrontation with its poor people. The finance minister pointed out that the last time a Mexican government preferred a confrontation, "We had a civil war with one million deaths." He was

Total Population and Percent Urban Population by Country, 1960 and 1980

	1960 Total	%Urban	1980 Total	%Urban
Argentina	20,611,000	74	27,720,000	85
Barbados	119,000	40	246,000	46
Bolivia	3,313,000	27	5,600,000	33
Brazil	70,758,000	46	120,287,000	68
Chile	7,701,000	68	11,104,000	82
Colombia	16,233,000	51	26,115,000	76
Costa Rica	1,254,000	33	2,223,000	46
Cuba	7,000,000	58	9,706,000	67
Dominican Republic	3,036,000	30	5,431,000	54
Ecuador	4,336,000	35	7,996,000	44
El Salvador	2,433,000	38	4,813,000	40
Guatemala	3,965,000	34	7,053,000	32
Guyana	578,000	30	849,000	47
Haiti	3,574,000	11	5,008,000	25
Honduras	1,895,000	23	3,691,000	36
Jamaica	1,613,000	24	2,247,000	69
Mexico	34,923,000	50	69,900,000	69
Nicaragua	1,420,000	38	2,422,000	58
Panama	1,062,000	42	1,837,000	54
Paraguay	1,710,000	35	3,168,000	37
Peru	10,022,000	46	17,624,000	71
Trinidad & Tobago	831,000	39	1,165,000	64
Uruguay	2,438,000	80	2,921,000	81
Venezuela	7,352,000	67	15,061,000	78
Latin America	208,336,000	50	354,287,000	66
United States	179,323,000	70	226,000,000	74

referring to the wars of the Mexican Revolution of 1910-1920.

THE URBAN SLUMS

The depth and extent of Latin America's poverty is easiest to see in its famous urban slums. These slums are called *turgurios* in Colombia, *ranchos* in Venezuela, *barriadas* in Peru, *callampas* in Chile, *villas miserias* in Argentina, and *favelas* in Brazil. This list does not exhaust the names or countries in which the slums appear. At their worst, cal-lampas, favelas, or barriadas are communities of people crowded together in one- or two-room shacks that often house families of six or eight members. The communities frequently lack toilets, sewers, running water, schools, health clinics, and often even electricity. Nevertheless, for the Latin Americans who live in them, these slums are solutions to the problem of trying to survive on little or no income.

The place is Lima, Peru in 1970. It is early in the morning. The air is cool, and the sky is overcast, as it nearly always is in Lima. Germán, who is twenty-two, married, and the father of two children, is awake and preparing to go to work. He is a bus driver. This morning he is not thinking about the long day ahead when he must drive the noisy, crowded bus. He is thinking about the secret move that he and his family will make that evening to a new home.

He currently lives in a small, two-room apartment in an old building near the center of Lima. The two rooms look out over a narrow, dark, littered alleyway. The lighting is poor, and there is never any fresh air. The water runs only a few hours each day, and the drains are clogged. The entire building is old and worn-down. It is noisy, crowded, bad smelling, and generally unhealthful. The neighborhood is filled with thieves, and acts of violence are common.

The secret move of Germán, his wife, and family has been planned carefully for over a month. Thirty-two families are involved. These families all have several things in common. At least one member of each family has migrated to Lima from a small town in the Andes; all are poor; all find their current housing and neighborhood unsatisfactory; all are convinced that by moving they will have a better place in which to live; and all believe that their standard of living will improve. None intends to leave Lima, bad as living conditions are. They certainly have no intention of returning to the kind of small Andean mountain town where many of them were born.

The secret plan calls for the thirty-two families to invade and occupy land on the outskirts of the city. They know the government is about to survey and divide this land into lots. Invasion and occupation is to take place at night. Each family, upon arrival, will quickly stake out and claim a small piece of land, then hurriedly erect a temporary one-room home. The floor will be the earth itself. The walls will be made of a woven straw matting attached to two-by-two-inch stakes. For the time being, no house will have a roof. A roofless house is not a great hardship, since rain almost never falls in Lima and the temperature is always mild. Of course, there will be no electricity, no running water, no plumbing, and no stores and shops. The group will, nevertheless, fight to hold the land and willingly suffer such missing necessities.

The lack of facilities will be temporary if the group clears the next hurdle, which involves negotiating with the government housing board. The families will have to persuade the housing board to accept the illegal invasion. They believe that they will be successful and that the board will then survey the land and assign lots to them. After this hurdle is overcome, each family will begin to construct a solid brick home on its lot. Eventually, water, electricity, and sewerage facilities will be installed. Shops and stores will appear. Schools and a public health clinic will be built. Bus lines will be extended to provide relatively cheap transportation into and around Lima. In this way, these families will find that they have changed from a group of people who joined together and illegally occupied land to an established community owning valuable property.

The place is Recife, Brazil, on the eastern coast of South America. The time is July 1979. Another urban invasion has taken place. On a Monday morning eight vans of police are summoned to protect the hilly land of the Vieira Cunha Construction Company. The property had been vacant, but over the weekend three hundred families consisting of more than one thousand people began to occupy it. The men, women, and children worked together day and night in a *mutirão*, or collective house-raising. This way, they needed only the weekend to construct most of the three hundred mud and stick dwellings. The police are greeted with stones and angry shouts. They react and threaten to destroy the mud huts. This angry confrontation causes a representative of the Church to enter as a peacemaker. Dom Helder Camara, the Archbishop of Recife, appears to ask that the invading families keep calm and not lose hope. "No violence. You are not alone. Even if what you have built is destroyed, do not react, because we are trying to find a solution for the problem."

A settlement is negotiated in which the invaders of what is now a new favela will pay a small monthly rent to the construction company. Later, the Archbishop comments that what happened "is proof that misery and hunger are invading the hills of Recife. It is no use to say that this is agitation and subversion. It is poverty, misery, entire families without a place to live who invade these empty lands."

The Latin American slums, for all they lack, are still a solution—not a problem—for their inhabitants. If governments will invest money and provide the necessary streets, sewers, toilets, running water, schools, health clinics, and recreation centers, these slums will be converted into desirable working-class neighborhoods. They can become a partial solution to urban poverty.

AGRARIAN REFORM

The people of Latin America continue to stream to cities, where schools, hospitals, money, and jobs are most plentiful. In 1960, one out of two Latin Americans lived in a town or city. By 1980, the ratio changed so that two out of three Latin Americans were town and city dwellers. The urban population more than doubled in twenty years. Nevertheless, one-third of the population continued to be rural. The absolute

(United Nations photo/Martin Pendl)

Swelling urban populations have produced high concentrations of people in areas with few resources or jobs.

numbers had increased from 101 to 116 million people. In nine countries—Bolivia, Costa Rica, Ecuador, El Salvador, Guatemala, Haiti, Honduras, Guyana, and Paraguay—the rural population remained a majority. The overwhelming majority of rural Latin American people are small landowners or peasants without land who work for others. Land and income are unequally divided. Three percent of the landowners possess sixty percent of the land. These are the owners of haciendas, fazendas, and plantations. In sharp contrast, roughly thirty percent of rural landowners hold about fifteen percent of the land in small plots called *minifundios*. By definition, the minifundio plot is too small to provide peasant owners and their families with more than a subsistence living. The income gap between the large estate (that is, the hacienda, fazenda, or plantation) and the minifundio is enormous. In 1960, the income of an average large estate was sixty-six times greater than that of the minifundio in Argentina, sixty-one times greater in Brazil, seventy-one times greater in Chile, 165 times greater in Ecuador, and four hundred times greater in Guatemala.

The largest group of rural Latin American people are those who own no land at all and must work for others who do. Landless peasants make up about forty-five percent of the rural population. The minifundio owners and landless farm workers make up the class of poor peasants. Between 1960 and 1980, this class grew faster than any rural group.

Rural inequality and poverty have been a growing threat to Latin America's social stability for more than a century. This period is roughly the same time as that covered by Latin America's industrial program. Since 1950, Latin Americans and foreigners who support industrialization have criticized the poor performance of the Latin American rural economy. They have agreed that the economy produced neither enough basic raw materials, such as wood and cotton, for local industries nor enough food for the growing populations in the cities. Nor did haciendas and minifundios use much labor-saving farm machinery, fertilizers, insecticides, or other products of industry.

City-based supporters of industrialization have tried to eliminate certain weaknesses they see in Latin American agriculture. They offer two solutions: The first is to provide more government and bank credit to landowners, so they can buy seeds, fertilizers, and farm machinery and undertake irrigation projects. Local industries will directly benefit because they produce many·or sometimes all of these items. The second is land reform. During the 1960s, most Latin American countries passed land reform laws. These laws typically left the hacienda with a core of two hundred to five hundred acres. Remaining land was sheared away and distributed among tenants. Sometimes lands were added to surrounding minifundios if these were deemed too small to support an owner and his family. Hacienda lands might also be added to a nearby Indian community from which they may have been taken a century earlier.

The land reform laws of the 1960s, though impressive on paper, were seldom applied. Land reform does not happen because city politicians or industrial groups manage to pass reform laws. Land reform that finally breaks up the haciendas has historically almost always come when the rural poor of Latin America demand it. The dream of the Latin American peasant is to have land sufficient to feed himself and his family and to establish for himself and them an economically stable and secure life. If he belongs to an Indian village community, his concern will be that the village has enough land for its people. Some examples will help us understand how the peasant contributes to making land reform a reality.

Mexico

In Morelos, Mexico, a mountain province located to the south of Mexico City, owners of haciendas were turning them into modern sugar plantations during the period from

1880-1910. They invested heavily in irrigation works and mills for grinding the cane. To pay for these investments, they needed to plant, harvest, and grind more sugar cane. Planting more cane required more land. Surrounding Indian villages began to lose lands to the hungry haciendas. Without lands, the villages could not survive. Many Morelos villages disappeared during this thirty-year period. They received no help from the government, which favored the hacendados' cause.

In the spring of 1910, the peasants of one village began to prepare their fields for planting. The local sugar hacienda owner claimed the fields, and his manager ordered the villagers off them. They were told to "plant in a flowerpot." Emiliano Zapata, a village leader, organized a group of eighty armed men and led the villagers back to the disputed fields. The hacienda manager, faced with this show of force, withdrew his workers, who were about to plant sugar cane. The villagers planted their corn. The Mexican Revolution (1910-1920) had begun, and Zapata became the principal leader of Mexico's land-hungry peasants until he was assassinated in 1919. The land reform program that finally destroyed the hacienda in Mexico began because peasants defended their interest with direct armed action.

Peru

In the early 1960s, the Peruvian government and army were confronted by a revolutionary guerrilla movement supported by peasants. By 1965 the movement had been defeated, but the victory was more difficult to win than the army had anticipated. In 1968, the Peruvian armed forces overthrew a civilian government. Still worried about a resurgence of peasant-supported guerrilla activities, the new military dictatorship decreed agrarian reform and began to distribute Andean hacienda lands to Indian communities and peasant families. Hundreds of thousands of Peru's rural poor benefitted from the law.

This Peruvian agrarian reform probably would not have occurred had it not been for the threat of a peasant armed revolt. That the reform was not completely to the satisfaction of Peru's peasants is demonstrated by the revival of guerrilla warfare in southern Peru during 1982 and 1983. The government admits that five hundred people were killed by guerrillas who belong to the *Sendero Luminoso* movement. The movement clearly has strong popular support in certain areas of rural Peru and also is able to disrupt life in the capital city of Lima by dynamiting electric power stations and killing public officials.

Bolivia

In 1951, the Bolivian army illegally cancelled the results of a presidential election. The winning party then passed out arms to its civilian supporters. In early 1952, an uprising toppled the government and virtually abolished the army. Indian communities and peasants took advantage of the disorders and seized hacienda lands, killing managers and owners who resisted. The new government had not anticipated a radical land reform but had to accept one in the face of peasant action. The peasant and Indian communities that acquired lands generally became a peaceful, satisfied political force.

These examples demonstrate that agrarian reform is successful when it is linked to peasant aspirations and peasant action. Wherever it has occurred, it has succeeded. When impoverished peasants receive land and fair wages or are freed from the hacienda servitude that makes them provide free labor to owners, they often become a satisfied, and even conservative, political force. The elimination of parasitic large landowners also increases productivity in the long run, though it may decrease output at first. In 1980, the revolutionary sponsors of Nicaragua's agrarian reform discovered that peasants who receive the lands of productive cotton or sugar plantations will plant beans and corn for their own needs before they will plant cotton and sugar for the Nicaraguan market or for export. If given money for seeds and fertilizers, they will spend it on shoes, shirts, and pants because they have almost no clothing. Nevertheless, Latin American peasants quickly assume responsibilities and function as one vital class in a complex rural-urban society. In 1983, a Brazilian peasant who headed a rural labor union told a group of university students that the greatest national problem was the fight over land. "Without land," he said, "peasants cannot plant corn, beans, and rice." He also pointed out that "the people of the country cannot live without the help of the people of the city. But people in the city cannot live without the help of the peasants who grow the food that everyone needs." If the two groups lend each other a helping hand, he said, "We can make a new world."

DEMOCRACY OR REVOLUTION?

During the colonial era, Latin American political power was in the hands of distant European monarchs and their ministers or the local officials whom they appointed. Laws and decisions were handed down and imposed on people. Since no other system of government existed, these laws were accepted by Latin Americans as long as they believed the king's government followed principles of justice. This justice did not extend to exploited masses of Indians and slaves who frequently rebelled. The power of the ruling Spanish and Portuguese imperial governments—backed by local privileged groups of landowners, merchants, mine owners, and churchmen—was strong enough to defeat these rebellions.

After independence, Latin Americans established new political systems. These systems had republican forms of government, usually inspired by the example of the United States. Republican governments meant that officials were elected for limited terms to represent the interests of the electors.

The political weakness of the Latin American independent republics was that they were controlled by a small, privileged minority of the population. Governments represented the interests of landowners, mine owners, and merchants. To these groups were later added industrialists and a small middle class. Roughly three-quarters of the population could not vote or hold office. They were excluded from the benefits of republican government.

Naturally, the policy of exclusion made Latin American societies politically unstable. Revolutions and uprisings became so frequent in some countries that they were routine events. Since groups of privileged Latin Americans were unwilling to give up the system of cheap or unpaid labor or to share their political rights with the larger population, they frequently looked to the armies for protection. Therefore, every Latin American republic suffered through one or more military dictatorships. Militarism became a constant in the region's political life. A Brazilian journalist once wrote that Latin American countries should elect war ministers, not presidents, since power resided in the army; the war minister could appoint the president of the republic to take care of certain government papers and fulfill ceremonial functions, knowing that he would be subject to instant dismissal.

In 1964, a military revolt in Brazil overthrew a democratic system that had lasted eighteen years. This revolt was the first of what became a cycle of military movements that struck down constitutional government in some of Latin America's richest countries. These included Peru (1968), Uruguay (1973), Chile (1973), and Argentina (1976).

The new military dictatorships quickly developed certain ideas that distinguished them from their predecessors. These ideas might be labeled the doctrine of national security. The military dictatorships of Brazil, Peru, Uruguay, Chile, and Argentina understood that the doctrine of national security gave them the right to eliminate all internal opposition. This opposition might include a guerrilla group that launched a war against the dictatorship, trade union leaders who defended the interests of workers, industrialists who criticized government economic policies, newspaper editors who criticized the dictatorship, or even priests and bishops who spoke against the terrible conditions of poverty.

The methods of "protecting" the national security that the military dictatorships used included press censorship, closing national legislatures, and kidnapping, torturing, or killing anyone believed to be an opponent. Perhaps some of the worst excesses of military violence in the name of national security occurred in Argentina between 1976 and 1981 when an estimated fifteen to thirty thousand Argentines "disappeared." These "disappeared" individuals were usually kidnapped and then either killed or kept secretly imprisoned.

Latin American military dictatorships that operated under a national security doctrine often excused their violence by arguing that a nation needed internal peace in order to develop its economy. The dictatorships were serious about making good records in economic development. They believed that high rates of economic growth could be a substitute for democracy. Furthermore, military commanders often believed that they were more competent to govern and direct an economy than the civilian politicians they overthrew. They were mistaken.

The severe economic recession that engulfed the free world in the early 1980s deeply affected Latin America's national economies. Prices for traditional Latin American exports such as sugar, iron ore, copper, and coffee fell by one-third. Throughout the 1970s, the military dictatorships had followed the examples of the democratic government they looked down on and borrowed billions of dollars from international banks. When prices and sales of exports fell, they could not repay their debts. Brazil's dictatorship led the list of Latin American and world borrowers, accumulating a foreign debt of $96 billion by the end of 1983. Brazil was followed by Mexico with $85 billion; Argentina with $43 billion; Venezuela with $27 billion; Chile with $20 billion; and Peru with $12 billion. Four of the six largest Latin American debtors—Argentina, Brazil, Chile, and Peru— could point to their military dictatorships as being responsible, or largely responsible, for the debts. These countries also had high unemployment rates. An estimated twenty-four percent of the economically active population of Argentina and Brazil were out of work, while the figures in Chile (thirty-two percent) and Peru (fifty-seven percent) were even higher. The Mexican and Venezuelan political democracies were also deeply in debt. However, Mexican (fifteen percent) and Venezuelan (two percent) rates of unemployment were significantly lower.

The dictatorships of Argentina and Chile were challenged by their people throughout 1983. One demonstration for democracy in Chile brought out a million people, despite a government threat to use force against the gathering. General strikes almost completely stopped work in Argentina three times in 1982 and 1983. The Argentine military government, having led the nation into a disastrous war against Great Britain over the control of the Malvinas Atlantic (Falkland) islands in 1982 and unable to prevent general strikes, finally gave up power.

Argentines reacted with a festival of democracy. They elected a new civilian president, Raul Alfonsin. Millions of Argentines filled the streets of Buenos Aires to celebrate the election. The celebration was greater than anything seen since 1978 when Argentina won the world soccer cup, the world's biggest sporting event. Evidently, the Argentines like democracy.

Latin American military dictatorships have always produced political instability. They excessively favor the interests of one group against those of another group. Those favored have usually been the Latin American upper and middle classes. The mistreated have generally been workers and peasants. Military dictatorships are not skillful at resolving big or small conflicts between groups, nor do they allow differences to be settled in free elections. Military dictatorships get political power through force, and they hold it through force. They give up power when confronted with the threat or reality of stronger force.

Contemporary Revolutions and Civil Wars

The majority of Latin Americans value democracy, liberty, and social justice—that is, they believe in free elections and representative government (democracy and liberty). Poor Latin Americans are also ready to travel anywhere in their countries in search of work or land, and they will labor for others if they are paid an adequate wage and are allowed to organize in defense of their own interests (liberty and social justice). Revolutions and violent civil wars occur because military dictatorships flagrantly violate one or all of the values of democracy, liberty, and social justice.

In 1944, a Cuban dictator soldier, Fulgencio Batista, voluntarily gave up the office of President of Cuba and went into exile. A freely elected democratic government succeeded Batista. Eight years later, the ex-dictator returned and staged a military revolt on the eve of another presidential election, which was cancelled.

Batista returned to power as a dictator backed by the army. He thereby opened the door to Fidel Castro, a law student and the son of a sugar planter, who at age twenty-six led an attack of young rebels on an army barracks. They hoped to overthrow Batista and restore democracy to Cuba. The attack failed. Castro himself was captured, tried, and convicted. Released from jail in 1954, he went into exile in Mexico. In 1956, he invaded Cuba with eighty-two men and

(United Nations photo/Y. Nagata)

The Communist revolution of Fidel Castro provoked profound changes in Cuban social structure and has given impetus to social revolutions elsewhere in Latin America.

started a guerrilla war against Batista. Operating out of the mountains in eastern Cuba and aided by other groups that opposed the Batista dictatorship, Castro triumphed in late 1958. He promised to restore democracy and carry out a series of reforms written into Cuba's 1940 Constitution. These included land reform (i.e., the abolition of the large estate) and turning foreign properties into Cuban properties.

The United States government resisted Castro's program of economic reform, which included seizing foreign-owned rural and urban properties. At first, Castro offered to pay all landowners, including foreigners, on the basis of the low property values they had reported to the previous Cuban government in order to avoid paying high taxes. Castro enjoyed this joke at the expense of the large landowners, but they were not amused and protested bitterly. When Castro nationalized United States-owned sugar mills, he offered to pay the owners with earnings from a special high price to be charged to United States purchasers of Cuban sugar.

In early 1961, the United States broke diplomatic relations with Cuba. Castro now felt free to pursue a course of open Communist revolution. Cuba gradually became a Communist dictatorship. Although the Cuban Communist state rejects democracy and liberty, it has striven for social justice. That is, all Cubans have work, and all working Cubans receive wages sufficient to pay for what they need. Castro's priorities are: education, health, jobs, and an adequate supply of such necessities as food, housing, and clothing. Communist Cuba's achievements include the elimination of urban slums, hunger, unemployment, and illiteracy. Cuba has set a standard for social justice virtually unknown in Latin America.

The Cuban Revolution began when a former dictator staged a military coup, cancelled elections, and eliminated democracy. The tragic, barbaric civil wars in Central America have developed for similar reasons. In 1934, the Nicaraguan National Guard, a substitute army, kidnapped and murdered the guerrilla leader, August Sandino, after he had laid down his guns and was negotiating with the government. Two years later, the commander of the National Guard, Anastasio Somoza, overthrew a constitutional government and established a personal, perpetual family dictatorship. Somoza's assassination in 1956 did not end family control. First one son, then a second, ruled as dictator president backed by the National Guard.

The Somoza family not only ruled Nicaragua; they virtually owned the country. In the 1970s, between one-fourth and one-third of all Nicaraguan means of production were controlled by this family. In the middle of the 1970s, the Somoza family fortune was estimated at $500 million, while total annual national income was approximately $2 billion.

Since the Somoza family did not allow free elections and assassinated or tried to buy off political opponents, popular armed resistance was inevitable. A National Liberation Sandinist Front (FSLN) made its initial guerrilla attack on a detachment of National Guardsmen in 1962. Seventeen years later, in 1979, a broad coalition of forces ended forty-two years of Somoza tyranny after a civil war that nearly destroyed the country.

Meanwhile, in neighboring El Salvador another civil war exploded. Its origins go back to the 1880s, when hacendados expanded their estates by devouring Indian peasant village lands. The hacendados wanted to grow more coffee for export. Indians who lost lands became landless farm workers. In December 1931, a military revolt gave the country a new army dictator. A month later, in January 1932, a peasant revolt erupted in the coffee zone. While suppressing the revolt, the Salvadorean army massacred nearly thirty thousand peasants. The landowner class abdicated power in favor of the army that had saved it. The massacre terrorized, but probably also united, the surviving peasants.

Forty years later, in 1972, a group of political parties competed in what was supposed to be a free election. The

Christian Democratic civilian candidate, José Napolean Duarte, was opposed by a general. The votes were miscounted, falsified, or destroyed so that the general might win. A popular uprising followed that included some members of the army. Guatemalan and Nicaraguan troops had to be summoned to help suppress the revolt.

Violent opposition developed against the Salvadorean military dictatorship that did not permit the political opposition to win a free election. The government responded with more violence. Special death squads—with the connivance of the army—assassinated peasants, workers, politicians, students, foreign agrarian reform experts, nuns, and even the Archbishop of San Salvador. El Salvador's class conflict had resulted in total violence that led to a murderous civil war in which compromise was not possible. El Salvador's civil war is likely to end only when one side defeats the other.

Yet another civil war was bringing death to thousands of Guatemalans. Many of the victims were Indian peasants. About half the Guatemalan population consists of Indians, and the savage deaths frequently inflicted on them gave this conflict the added dimension of a race war.

The beginnings of the Guatemalan civil war go back to the events of 1944 and 1945. In 1945, a reforming civilian government, which had been elected with eighty percent of the votes and was headed by Juan José Arevalo, succeeded a military dictatorship overthrown in 1944 during a revolt of workers and students. Six years later, in 1950, Guatemalans choose another president, Jacobo Arbenz. He received sixty percent of the votes. In 1954, opponents of the government, led by a group of army officers, invaded Guatemala from neighboring Honduras and drove Arbenz—and democracy—out of Guatemala. The United States Central Intelligence Agency (CIA) helped plan the invasion. The United States government had been angered because Guatemala nationalized some of the properties of the United Fruit Company and legalized the Communist party.

The new Guatemalan government was an anti-Communist, military dictatorship. In 1963, a president general who promised free elections was toppled by the army because he intended to allow former reform president Juan José Arevalo to run for office. The rebellious army then cancelled the upcoming elections. In the presidential elections of 1970, 1974, and 1978, only generals could run for office. Individuals labeled as "unacceptable" opponents did not have the right to compete for any offices. Naturally, the majority of Guatemalans had no reason to vote. Only ten percent of the adult population voted for the winning general in 1970. By 1978, the figure had fallen to eight percent. In 1980, the reform-oriented Christian Democratic party, the most important civilian opposition party, closed its headquarters and announced there was no longer any reason to participate in Guatemalan politics. Clearly, political questions would be decided by bullets, not ballots.

Meanwhile, army officers were growing rich. During the 1970s, the army established its own development bank. Army officers also became large landowners. In one instance, a group of army officers seized land that was supposed to be given to peasants under an agrarian reform program.

Violence increased in the late 1970s. In 1979, a group of Indians were invited to come to a small town to discuss their land claims. When they arrived, waiting soldiers fired on them, killing 119. In 1980, another group of Indians went to the Spanish embassy in Guatemala City. They wanted to draw attention to the kidnapping and murder of Indians in the northern part of Guatemala. Soldiers arrived and demanded that the embassy turn the Indians over to them. The embassy refused, and the soldiers attacked, setting fire to the building and killing the entire delegation of protestors. The Spanish ambassador himself was wounded in the assault, which was a total violation of international law. Pro-government, private army death squads operate as freely as in El Salvador. One

day in 1983, the Guatemalan president stated that the
Catholic Church contained subversive priests. The next day
a death squad killed a priest. During 1982 and 1983, an
estimated fifteen thousand Guatemalans were assassinated
by death squads.

THE PRESENT AND FUTURE OF LATIN AMERICA

In trying to predict the future of Latin America, two new
factors need to be noted. First, the Latin American people,
especially poor Latin Americans, are more organized and
better prepared to struggle for what they want than ever
before. Nothing is easier in any Latin American nation than
to organize reform political parties with a mass of supporters.
However, when the armed forces do not allow citizens to
organize or vote, some opponents of the dictatorship are
driven to create revolutionary guerrilla movements. After a
few military successes, they attract a following of sympa-
thizers or active militants.

The second new factor is the changing role of the Church.
In 1954, the Archbishop of Guatemala blessed the invasion
that overthrew a democratically-elected government and set
up a military dictatorship. In the 1980s, the Guatemalan
army labeled priests "subversives" and allowed death squads
to kill them. Evidently, the thinking of people inside the Latin
American Catholic Church has changed since the 1950s. In
1968 at Medellin, Colombia, and again in 1979 at Puebla,
Mexico, the Church officially took out an option in favor of
the poor, condemning conditions that led to poverty. Trans-
lated into policy, this meant that the Church in Brazil could
defend hungry people who invade supermarkets and take
food. In 1983 when the São Paulo chief of police said that he
might order his officers to shoot looters, the Cardinal
Archbishop of São Paulo responded that bullets were not the
solution for hunger and unemployment. Each Sunday, the

Archbishop of San Salvador announces the preceding week's death toll in his nation's civil war. He has urged foreign governments, including the United States government, to stop the flow of guns to El Salvador as the first step to de-escalating his country's civil war. In 1983, the Archbishop of Santiago, Chile, demanded that the ruling military dictatorship dissolve its secret police force.

A Brazilian peasant fighting to keep his land says that a big change has come over the Church. "Before the priests were against us. Now each day they are more in solidarity with us." It is clear that the Church favors democracy and social justice in Latin America. The Archbishop of Recife, Helder Camara, insists on the importance of the latter: "Without social justice, peace is just a pretty word."

In the 1980s, Latin America was clearly at a turning point. A twenty-year cycle of military dictatorships seemed to be approaching an end. Military officers in power had not solved the problem of Latin American poverty. In fact, under military dictatorships poverty seemed to increase more than under democracies. Military dictatorships were certainly less able to cope with the effects of the world economic crisis of the early 1980s. Crushing foreign debt payments, high inflation, and rising unemployment became serious social problems that the unelected and repressive Argentine and Chilean dictatorships could not solve. These governments were under siege, attacked by their own people. The Argentine dictatorship was finally driven from power.

Military dictatorships almost never have the political skills to negotiate agreements with opponents in time of crisis. The stubborn refusal of the dictatorships in Nicaragua, Guatemala, and El Salvador to allow social conflicts and tensions to be resolved by democratic procedures turned these Central American nations into zones of terrible civil war in the late 1970s and early 1980s. Between 1978 and 1983, one hundred thousand people have died in these Central American wars, according to the Archbishop of San Salvador. It is interesting that the small Central American nation of Costa Rica, immediately to the south of Nicaragua, has been spared these wars. In 1948, Costa Rica took the road to democracy. It abolished its army and has had regular elections ever since. Social peace is a constant in Costa Rica. Its people are the best educated and most prosperous in Central America.

For the vast majority of Latin Americans, there are only two political choices in the 1980s: democracy or revolution. Military dictatorships, always unstable, have been shown to be incompetent, violent, inflexible, and unpopular. But, while democracy or revolution remain the two political choices, the urgent social issue is how to overcome poverty. There is no easy solution for poverty in a free democracy. It is clear that the majority of Latin Americans want to try to eliminate poverty by non-violent, democratic means. Whether or not they will have the chance remains the great unanswered question.

QUESTIONS
FOR DISCUSSION

CHAPTER 1

1. Should the geography of Latin America be thought of as an obstacle to human settlement and the creation of societies and civilizations?
2. Present-day Latin Americans are the descendants of what peoples?
3. Compare the "melting pot" process of Latin America with that of the United States.

CHAPTER 2

1. What types of societies did the Indian and African peoples possess?
2. How were the Indians, Africans, and Europeans brought together in colonial Latin America? What roles did each group play?
3. During the colonial period, to which group of people would you want to belong? Why? Is there any group to which you would not want to belong? Why?
4. Today's Latin America has been called a society without political democracy and individual equality. Was this also true for the colonial period?

CHAPTER 3

1. Would you say that independence brought many changes to Latin America? If so, what were they? What did not change?

2. Did the independence period produce a Latin American social revolution? Discuss.

3. Some people would argue that the Palmares runaway slave communities created a Latin American social revolution and that Paraguay from 1813 to 1864 achieved true political and economic independence. Are these people correct? Why or why not?

CHAPTER 4

1. How has the idea of economic growth and development in Latin America changed since independence?

2. How have private Latin American capital, governments, and foreign investors contributed to Latin American industrialization?

3. Discuss the strength and weakness of Latin American programs for economic growth and development.

4. Are you impressed with the record of economic development in Latin America? Why or why not?

CHAPTER 5

1. Describe a Latin American urban slum. How can it be thought of as a solution rather than a problem?

2. In your opinion, how serious is the problem of poverty in Latin America? Do you think that poverty is a threat to peace in Latin America? Why or why not?

3. Discuss the difference between a military dictatorship and a democracy in Latin America. Which system do you think is better for Latin America? Why?

4. How can it be argued that present-day Latin America is passing through a crisis?

GLOSSARY

Aguardiente A strong, popular Latin American alcoholic beverage.

Arawaks A Caribbean Indian people discovered by the Spaniards in the 1490s and exterminated within fifty years of being discovered; a first, overwhelming proof of the inability of native Americans to withstand European power and diseases.

Aztecs An Indian people who organized an empire in Mexico between 1430 and 1519 when Spanish conquistadores entered Mexico and destroyed it (1519-1521).

Balmaceda, José Manuel President of Chile (1886-1891) who favored local industrialization and who fought with Chile's legislature. Defeated in a civil war, he committed suicide.

Bandeirantes Indian slave hunters, gold hunters, and explorers of the Brazilian wilderness during the colonial period. The bandeirantes came from Sao Paulo.

Batista, Fulgencio Cuban President (1940-1944) and dictator (1952-1958). Batista was overthrown by a popular revolution led by Fidel Castro between 1956 and 1958.

Bolívar, Simón (1783-1830) Venezuelan soldier and independence leader who helped liberate and create five Latin American nations (Venezuela, Colombia, Ecuador, Peru, and Bolivia).

Castro, Fidel Guerrilla leader and revolutionary who came to power in Cuba in 1959 after having led a popular revolution against the dictator Fulgencio Batista. Castro has maintained himself in power since 1959, and under his leadership, Cuba has become an important Communist state.

Compadrazgo A form of godparenthood, widespread in Latin America.

Conquistador A mounted, Spanish warrior. A few hundred conquistadores were largely responsible for the destruction of the Aztec and Inca empires, which consisted of millions of people.

Encomienda A system by which conquered Indians entrusted to Spaniards received instruction in the Christian religion and in return had to contribute labor and commodity tribute.

Francia, Jose Gaspar Rodrigues De (1766-1840) Paraguayan leader (1811-1840) who isolated his country from the rest of the world and led it to prosperity and independence.

Great Escarpment A two-thousand-mile-long mountainous slope fronting the coast of much of Brazil.

Greater Antilles A group of large islands (Cuba, Jamaica, Puerto Rico, and Hispaniola, which contains the two nations of Haiti and the Dominican Republic) that comprise the West Indies in the Caribbean.

Grito de Dolores The 1810 "cry" or shout of Mexican independence.

Hacienda The large, generally underproductive Latin American farm or large estate. Usually worked by landless peasant tenants who accepted the authority of the owner, performed certain unpaid services for him, and in return received the right to cultivate a small parcel of hacienda land. Called the fazenda in Brazil.

Hidalgo y Costilla, Miguel White priest who led mestizos and Indians in the Mexican uprising for independence in 1810.

Incas The Incas were native Americans who organized a vast empire of millions of people in Peru and were destroyed by a Spanish conquistador invasion during the years 1533 to 1535.

Lopez, Francisco Solano Paraguayan leader who lead his nation into a disastrous war against Argentina, Brazil, and Uruguay between 1864 and 1870.

Mayans Indians who created a civilization in southern Mexico and Central America before the arrival of Europeans.

Mestizo A Latin American with Indian and European ancestors and parents.

Miscegenation Biological mixture or interbreeding of the African, European, and Indian peoples.

Mita Inca labor tax, which required subject peoples to maintain roads, bridges, public buildings, etc. Adopted by Spanish rulers to force Peruvian and Bolivian Indians to maintain roads or to work in mines and textile mills.

Mulatto A Latin American with African and European ancestors and parents.

Multinational A corporation that has companies or investments in more than one country.

Palmares A group of runaway slaves who formed free communities in seventeenth-century Brazil.

Patiño, Simon (1864-1947) Bolivian owner of tin mines and one of the wealthiest men of his time.

PEMEX Mexican state owned oil monopoly company created in 1938 after the nationalization of British and United States oil properties.

PETROBRAS Brazil's state owned oil company organized in 1953.

Peon A Latin American agricultural worker or peasant usually attached to an hacienda.

Rio de la Plata An arm of the sea separating Argentina and Uruguay, into which flows the Parana and Uruguay rivers.

San Martin, Jose de (1778-1828) Argentine general who led armies to victories in the Latin American wars for independence, playing a particularly important role in the liberation of Chile and Peru from Spanish rule.

Somoza The family that ruled and plundered Nicaragua between 1937 and 1978.

Tienda de Raya   The hacienda company store. Peasants attached to the hacienda often had no choice except to purchase certain supplies at the tienda de raya at high prices set by the hacendado.

Transfer of Technology   Costly process by which companies sell or lease know-how, patents, formulas, and equipment to other companies. Latin Americans believe that transfer of technology fees paid to overseas multinational companies are usually too high.

Tupinamba   A general name to coastal Indians of Brazil, whom the Portuguese encountered when they arrived in 1550 and after.

Vodun   Popular religion brought by slaves from Africa to Haiti. Better known in the United States as voodoo. Afro-Brazilian versions are called Candomble, Macumba, and Xango.

Yucatan Peninsula   An area of southern Mexico and Guatemala. The Mexican part extends north into the Gulf of Mexico.

Zambo   A Latin American with African and Indian ancestors or parents.

SUGGESTED RESOURCE MATERIAL

GENERAL

Books

A few solid general books may be read by those wishing to increase their knowledge of Latin America quickly. Recommended are George Pendle, *A History of Latin America* (Baltimore, 1963); Frank Tannenbaum, *Ten Keys to Latin America* (New York, 1962); Charles Wagley, *An Introduction to Brazil* (New York, 1971); Hubert Herring, *A History of Latin America* (New York, 1968); and Paul Goodwin, Global Studies: Latin America (Guilford, CT 1984).

Periodicals

The National Geographic. This magazine has several superb, handsomely illustrated articles on Latin America each year.

CHAPTER 1

Bohannan, Paul. *Africa and the Africans* (New York, 1964).
Herring, Hubert. *A History of Latin America* (New York, 1968).
    Has useful, well-written chapters on the Indian, African, and European (i.e., the Spanish and Portuguese) backgrounds to Latin American history.
Herskovits, Melville J. *Life in a Haitian Valley* (New York, 1971).
James, Preston. *Latin America* (New York, 1969).
    Expertly covers all aspects of Latin America's geography.
Knight, Franklin W. *The African Dimension in Latin American Societies* (New York, 1974).
Mason, J. Alden. *The Ancient Civilizations of Peru* (Baltimore, 1957).

Sauer, Carl Ortwin. *The Early Spanish Main* (Berkeley, 1969).
Analyzes the organization of Indian society in the Caribbean
as well as the destructive impact of the Spanish conquest.
Vaillant, George C. *The Aztecs of Mexico* (New York, 1966).
Wagley, Charles. *An Introduction to Brazil* (New York, 1971).

CHAPTER 2

Boxer, Charles R. *The Golden Age of Brazil: 1695-1750*
(Berkeley, 1962).
An exciting book on Brazilian slavery in colonial Latin
America.
Diffie, Bailey W. *Latin American Civilization* (New York, 1967).
Gibson, Charles. *Spain in America* (New York, 1966).
Hemming, John. *The Conquest of the Incas* (New York, 1970).
_____. *Red Gold, The Conquest of the Brazilian Indians*
(Cambridge, 1978).
Herring, Hubert. *A History of Latin America* (New York, 1968).
The most readable account of the colonial period.
Kirkpatrick, F.A. *The Spanish Conquistadores* (New York,
1962).
A general history of the Spanish conquests.
MacLeod, Murdo J. *Spanish Central America: A Socioeconomic
History, 1520-1720* (Berkeley, 1973).
Morner, Magnus. *Race Mixture in the History of Latin America*
(Boston, 1967).
Padden, R.C. *The Hummingbird and the Hawk* (Columbus,
1967).
An engrossing interpretation of the Spanish defeat of the
Aztecs.
Tannenbaum, Frank. *Slave and Citizen* (New York, 1947).
Wagley, Charles and Marvin Harris. *Minorities in the New World*
(New York, 1958).

CHAPTER 3

Foner, Philip S. *The Spanish-Cuban-American War, 1895-
1902,* Volumes I and II (New York, 1972).

Hamill, Hugh. *The Hidalgo Revolt: Prelude to Mexican Independence* (Gainesville, 1966).
One of the best explanations of the Hidalgo movement.
James, C.L.R. *The Black Jacobins* (New York, 1963).
Presents a stirring account of Haiti's struggle for independence along with the life of Toussaint L'Ouverture, the principal leader of the struggle.
Johnson, John J. *The Military and Society in Latin America* (Stanford, 1964).
Tells of the rise and importance of the Latin American military.
————. *Simon Bolivar and Spanish American Independence* (Princeton, 1968).
Contains a brief biography and some of the major speeches and letters of Bolivar.
Mecham, J. Lloyd. *Church and State in Latin America* (Chapel Hill, 1966).
A look at church-state tensions and relationships.
Robertson, William Spence. *The Rise of the Spanish American Republics as Told in the Lives of Their Liberators* (New York, 1918).
Stein, Stanley and Barbara. *The Colonial Heritage of Latin America* (New York, 1970).
A summary of what colonialism left Latin America.
Trend. J.B. *Bolivar and the Independence of Spanish America* (London and New York, 1965).

CHAPTER 4

Benham, F., and H.A. Holley. *A Short Introduction to the Economy of Latin America* (London, 1960).
Dean, Warren. *The Industrialization of São Paulo* (Austin, 1969).
Evans, Peter. *Dependent Development: The Alliance of Multinational, State, and Local Capital in Brazil* (Princeton, 1979).
Furtado, Celso. *Economic Development of Latin America* (Cambridge, 1970).

Gordon, Wendell. *The Political Economy of Latin America* (New York, 1965).

Hanson, Simon G. *Economic Development in Latin America* (Washington, 1951).

Sarmiento, Domingo Faustino. *Life in the Argentine Republic* (various editions).

Stark, Harry. *Social and Economic Frontiers in Latin America* (Dubuque, 1961).

CHAPTER 5

Alves, Marcio Moreira. *A Grain of Mustard Seed: The Awakening of the Brazilian Revolution* (New York, 1973).

Anderson, Thomas P. *Matanza, El Salvador's Communist Revolution* (Lincoln, 1971).

Bell, John Patrick. *Crisis in Costa Rica* (Austin, 1971).

Debray, Regis. *The Chilean Revolution—Conversations with Allende* (New York, 1971).

_____. *Revolution in the Revolution* (New York, 1967).

Has been described as a textbook for revolutions in Latin America.

Dobyns, Henry E. and Paul L. Doughty. *Peru, A Cultural History* (New York, 1976).

Galeano, Eduardo. *Open Veins of Latin America* (New York, 1973).

A Latin American intellectual tries to explain the poverty of his region.

Gettleman, Marvin, et al., (eds). *El Salvador: Central America in the New Cold War* (New York, 1981).

Greene, Mary Francis and Orletta Ryan. *The Schoolchildren* (New York, 1965).

Takes the reader into a poor village in Ecuador in the 1960s.

Guevera, Ernesto "Che." *Venceremos* (New York, 1968).

Speeches and writings of one of Castro's chief lieutenants and a leading proponent of revolution in Latin America. Guevara was killed in Bolivia in 1967 while practicing what he preached.

Gunther, John. *Inside South America* (New York, 1966).
A popular, well-written book full of memorable details and interesting anecdotes.

Jesus, Carolina Maria de. *Child of the Dark* (New York, 1962).

Klein, Herbert. *Bolivia, the Evolution of a Multinational Society* (New York, 1982).

Knight, Franklin W. *The Caribbean, Genesis of Fragmented Nationalism* (New York, 1978).

Lernoux, Penny. *Cry of the People* (New York, 1980).
Information on the new Latin American Catholic Church.

Levinson, Jerome and Juan de Onis. *The Alliance That Lost Its Way* (Chicago, 1971).
Documents the history and failures of the Alliance of Progress.

Levy, Daniel C. and Gabriel Szekely. *Mexico, Paradoxes of Stability and Change* (Boulder, 1983).

Lewis, Oscar. *Five Families* (New York, 1959).

Lockwood, Lee. *Castro's Cuba, Cuba's Fidel* (New York, 1967).
One of the first long interview books with Fidel Castro.

Logan, Rayford W. *Haiti and the Dominican Republic* (New York, 1968).

Lombardi, John V. *Venezuela: The Search for Order, the Dream of Progress* (New York, 1982).

Loveman, Brian. *Chile: The Legacy of Hispanic Capitalism* (New York, 1979).

Meyer, Michael and William L. Sherman. *The Course of Mexican History* (New York, 1979).

Perlman, Janice E. *The Myth of Marginality: Urban Poverty and Politics in Rio de Janeiro* (Berkeley, 1976).

Poppino, Rollie. *Brazil, The Land and People* (New York, 1978).

Reed, John. *Insurgent Mexico* (1969).

Scobie, James R. *Argentina, A City and a Nation* (New York, 1971).

Thomas, Hugh. *Cuba, The Pursuit of Freedom* (New York, 1971).

Womack, John. *Zapata and the Mexican Revolution* (New York, 1968).

Woodward, Ralph Lee. *Central America, A Nation Divided* (New York, 1976).

PERIODICALS

Daily newspapers, weekly news magazines, and television news programs report the more dramatic events taking place in Latin America. For up-to-date facts and figures about the current scene in each country, consult the annual volumes of *The Statesman's Yearbook*. A valuable yearly publication of the Inter-American Development Bank is its *Socio-Economic Progress in Latin America*. Your library can obtain a free copy by writing the Bank of Washington, D.C. The United Nations publishes many pamphlets and documents about Latin America. Outstanding is the annual volume of the United Nations Economic Commission for Latin America (ECLA), entitled "Economic Survey of Latin America." The General Secretariat of the Organization of American States, 19th Street and Constitution Avenue, N.W., Washington, D.C. 20006, publishes different materials about Latin America, some of which will be sent free of charge. The North American Congress on Latin America (NACLA) publishes well-documented, controversial books and reports on Latin America.

AUDIO-VISUAL

Films can be magnificent experiences. A memorable documentary is *A Roof of Their Own* made by John Turner in Lima, Peru. In it, Turner filmed an actual slum invasion. *Black Orpheus* is a captivating film of Rio de Janeiro's poor at carnival time. For background, it uses some of the more picturesque slums of Rio whose life is made to seem unnaturally attractive and appealing. On the other hand, Luis Bunuel's *Los Olvidados (The Forgotten Ones)* shows the violence and inhumanity of a modern Latin American city. *El Alambrista (The Fence Jumper)* is the well-told, well-directed story of an undocumented Mexican migrant worker in the United States. A film about Cuba's Fidel Castro entitled *Fidel* is worth seeing.

INDEX

African slaves: contribution of, 18-
19; rebellions of, 36-40
Argentina: foreign debt of, 94; government corporation in, 63;
industrialization in, 58; military
violence in, 93
Argentine Institute for the Promotion
of Exchange (IAPI), 63, 64
agrarian reform: 85, 87-88; in Bolivia,
90-91; in Mexico, 88-89; in Peru,
89-90
agriculture: lake, 16; techniques of
New World Indians, 14, 16, 17
Amazon basin, 3, 6
Andes, 5
Arawak Indians, agricultural tech-
niquues of, 14, 16
armed forces: as political power, 48;
see also, military dictatorship
Asians, migration of, 9
Aztecs: 13; agricultural techniques
of, 16

Balmaceda, José Manuel, 29, 73, 74
banana plantations, of Guatemala, 54
bandeirantes, 50
barriadas, 82, 83
Batista, Fulgencio, 95, 97
black slaves: 9, 18, 19; rebellions of,
36-40
Bolivia: 5; land reform in, 90-91; tin
industry of, 55-57
Brazil: 40; Amazon basin in, 6; foreign debt of, 94; government role
in oil industry of, 65, 66; government role in steel industry of, 64;
independence of, 35; industrialization in São Paulo, 58-60; unemployment in, 79; urban invasion of Recife, 84-85; war with
Paraguay, 44, 45

callampas, 82, 83
Caribbean Islands, Indians of, 9, 14,
16
Castro, Fidel, 95, 97
Catholic Church: during colonial
period, 29-31; see also, Church;
religion

Central America: geography of, 5;
independence of, 35; poverty in,
80
Chile: 40; foreign debt of, 94; government corporation in, 63-64;
government role in steel industry
of, 64; industrialization in, 58;
legislature of, 29; unemployment
in, 79
Church: changing role of, 101-102;
role of, under colonial rule, 27, 29;
relationship of, with state, 30; see
also, Catholic Church; religion
civil wars, 95-101
coffee huller, invention and manufacture of, 59-60
Colombia: 40; legislature of, 29; steel
mill in, 64-65
colonial rule: 13, 19; Church's role
during, 29-31; exploitation during,
19-27; labor system under, 36;
political system under, 27, 29
compadrazgo, 25
computers, Brazilian-made vs. multinational-made, 76
Corporacion de Fomento
(FOMENTO), 63, 64
Costa Rica, peace and democracy in,
103
cruzeiros, 27
Cuba, Castro's program of economic
reform for, 97

democracy, vs. revolution, 91-95
Duarte, José Napolean, 99

economic development: and foreign
investment, 67-73; income distribution from, 79-80; phases of,
52-64; impact of, on poor, 77-78;
as present priority, 50
electricity, see hydroelectric power
ELECTROBRAS, 66
El Salvador, civil war in, 98-99, 101
encomienda, 20
Europeans: migration of, 9; political
control under, 13, 19
exploitation, during colonial period,
19-22

116